J. CORREDOR-MATHEOS

MIRÓ'S POSTERS

Catalogue of the posters by

GLORIA PICAZO

CHARTWELL BOOKS INC.

Translated from Spanish by Anita Roberts

Published by Chartwell Books Inc.
A Division of Book Sales Inc.
110 Enterprise Avenue
Secaucus, New Jersey 07094

ISBN 0-89009-360-1
Library of Congress Catalog Card Number: 80-81161

SUMMARY

THE PUBLISHER
Wishes to thank Galerie Maeght of Paris, Galeria Maeght of Barcelona and Mr Nils Tryding of Ahüs, Sweden, for the posters they have so kindly let us have to complete the catalogue of posters by Joan Miró.

Joan Miró and the poster

A concrete approach, such as this one, to Joan Miró's work offers several levels of interest, firstly in that it refers to the production of a great artist. Miró has been studied from many angles by numerous authors, and it was necessary that this area of his work also be studied. This reason alone could suffice. But there are more. The very fact of its being a sideline to the main current of his work allows us to penetrate Miró's world stealthily, taking it by surprise. A poster is not necessarily first and foremost a *work of art*. It comes into being for a purpose: it is, therefore, *applied* art. A poster by Miró will be used to make something known or to disseminate information, which in his case is cultural, an exhibition of his own or of another, a book, a congress, etc., but at the same time it is what is expected of him, it is *a Miró* and must be recognised as such. At the same time as it refers to something else, he himself, as an artist, is involved. This double role at least lightens the responsibility that the artist feels when faced with the blank canvas or paper, and which is particularly accentuated in Miró. However spontaneous they may appear, and actually are, his forms and symbols have demanded an absolute, conscious, reflective attention which neither curbs nor cools down the intuition, but which rather determines and perfects it. For this reason, the poster introduces an element of *distraction* (it is not the absolutely independent creation that constitutes the *work of art* that allows us to slip unnoticed into Miró's world.

There are other points to be considered, such as the possibilities offered to this artist to develop his particular leaning towards graphic work. A poster has to allow for rapid reading, not only of textual content but also of the whole, including the aesthetic factor. Because, as F. Enel writes, "more than a text to be read, the poster is above all an image imprinted on our minds without requiring the active participation of our consciousness", since, as this specialist goes on to say, "the image operates on the same level as the form" (1). Here we have, then, in the very heart of the world of Miró, a form converted into symbols, with frequent animal or vegetable analogies, which will here take the shape of figures of letters and numbers, those required by the aim of the poster. The fact that the commissions Miró has received — and accepted — are exclusively cultural, naturally strengthens his possibilities and allows the results to fit harmoniously into his world, to such an extent that they demand our attention and justify being dealt with in a monograph.

This book is a collection of Joan Miró's posters produced over a period of sixty years. The intensity of his work in this respect has been extremely diverse. From the first of them, for the Catalan magazine *L'Instant* — which was never published — to the next, there passed a period of eighteen years. This second poster did achieve circulation, and very much so. This was the famous *Aidez L'Espagne,* published (in 1937) in dramatic circumstances. We then have to leap forward another ten years to 1947, when we find the poster intended for the International Surrealist Exhibition in Paris. But this time the time lapse was fundamentally due to the Second World War. Thus we see that in 1948 he produces another poster for the exhibition in the Galerie Maeght. Miró's poster-producing activity has since then been very intense, and it was by no means purely fortuitous that, in 1963, he was commissioned to design the cover for a folder of fifty-two posters by different outstanding artists (2).

Some of his posters have been published in catalogues and books, and a large number of them brought together in Ralph Herrmanns' monograph *Affischer av Miró,* brought out in Stockholm in 1974. The present intention has been to put together all Miró's posters with a commentary to analyse their peculiar characteristics and values, at the same time relating them to his *œuvre* as a whole. The criterion has been to include only those created as actual posters, excluding the ones taken from the artist's paintings and drawings without his direct collaboration. This seems to us essential, in so far as it limits the topic to what Miró has actually contributed to this field, so frequently found in the collective life of our era.

Miró's posters may be taken from original lithographs — and in this case a printing is always made *avant la lettre* or from a gouache or sketch. Owing to the large number of posters of the former kind, the poster-producing side of Miró's work continues to bear a clear relation to his lithography in general, as can be confirmed on consulting the series of books entitled *Joan Miró lithographe* (3). It is worth noticing that some posters have the text written entirely in Miró's handwriting, whereas in others it is completely or partially in printed type. The relevance of this lies in the fact that, on occasion, the words required by the theme give Miró the opportunity to develop his graphic talent and in some way thereby to complete the global image. The fact that his colours are primary, flat hues shortens the distance that usually exists between the different techniques and serves to underline, in the case of the posters, their general connection with the lithographs. It is not a question of an isolated case, and we can see that Attilio Rossi, in his book *I Manifesti,* says with regard to the publication of *102 affiches by various artists,* printed by Mourlot: "We are dealing with genuine art lithographs which have experienced not only mechanical reproduction but also the delicacy of chromolithography". The result of this is the dominance of "the autographic stroke of the artist and the exquisiteness of his palette in a kind of blessed repose" (4).

The first posters: the shaping of a new language

The posters are firstly lyrical, with the enchanting chromatic poetry that was to catch on in the forties as a result of the free, unrestrained search for individual identity via inner roads. There is, however, one important exception: the previously mentioned *Aidez l'Espagne,* with the enormous clenched fist and the red and yellow on a blue background. The violence projected by this image is intermingled with joy; we seem to be able to read this in the colour and the hope which, more than hatred, upholds the arm, when the war is still following an upward trend.

The remaining posters of this period do not try to leap out and seize us as we go by: rather they count on our stopping before them and they are confident — with the self-confidence Miró has always shown — that they will *captivate* us. The are usually set in a surround, or at least with well-defined limits, emphasised occasionally by dotted edges and spots of colour: seen as a whole it bears some resemblance to a brightly-patterned handkerchief, with the carefree, *irresponsible* gaiety of absolute freedom. Miró produces his first posters without giving too much thought to the effect they will have as actual posters — remembering of course that Miró always takes this very much into account —, concerned solely with the plastic result. His themes are basically the same as in his painting at that time, that is, simplified: everything has to be as straightforward as possible. The poster of the Galerie Maeght exhibition in 1948 is very explicit in this respect. The theme of his figures should be included in the series of *women and birds* from the years immediately preceding this, and only just before those diagrammatic and magically poetic figures, along with what Dupin calls the "spontaneous" paintings of 1949-1950, become the symbols of a new alphabet. 1948 is also significant to the theme in hand because it marks the beginning of his work in the Mourlot *atelier*. And, related to all of this, in his connection with Maeght, who will be claiming his help to produce posters for his exhibitions and other displays connected with the Gallery.

The evolution of the Miró poster takes us from the integrated and unitary forms which began with the planned poster for the magazine *L'Instant,* in 1919, and continued in the *Aidez L'Espagne* poster in 1937, to more *liberated* compositions with independent elements but following a still determinant superior order. An example of this intermediate stage could be the one for the Miró exhibition at the Galerie Matarasso in Nice in 1957. The spatial distortion, which we notice the following year in the advertisement for Paul Eluard's book *À toute épreuve,* emphasises, in its deliberate instability, a period of searching. We must remember that between 1954 and 1959 he did not paint a single canvas, concentrating his attention on new or hitherto little-used techniques which allow him to abolish frontiers. It is the phase when he devotes his time intensely to ceramics, in collaboration with Llorens Artigas, to prints, lithographs and sculptural experiments. As Giuseppe Marchiori was to remark, this long parenthesis led "to new spatial solutions, the simplification of images within a new relation between the signs, lines, and the painted surface" (5).

The poster for the exhibition where he presented the book *Constellations,* with the reproduction of the works that make up the series of this name and twenty-two poems by André Breton in 1959, is a step forward in the relaxation of form. But it is all contained within an ovoid outline; the form that symbolically seems most suitable for enclosing another; whereas the following year's poster for the Maeght exhibition is now totally *non-formal*: pure colour splashes with blurred edges, a skein of intertwined lines and letters which jump around as if tending, with their movement, towards a *distortion* of their meaning. This is the latest colourist poster, with splashes of Miró's basic colours, red, yellow, blue and green, plus black, containing an element of compulsive self-identification.

Calligraphy and aggression

Reference must be made to the change recorded in his work towards 1960, with the introduction of black as the dominant colour. Henceforth, it will not only be used to emphasize forms, spatter or cross the surface with fine lines: its role will be to trace the theme and shape the form. The other colours will fill in the gaps, lacking the courage to counter the dark soul of what is the negation of all colour. This is what is noticeable in his work as a whole, and perhaps in a special way in his posters. The shock element of black is suitable for that impact the poster must have on the passer-by. For the poster's function is to attract attention, and black marks out, not just vigorously but with aggressiveness, the outlines and forms.

The clear distinction between figures and background is lost, and the space is bespattered with stains, joining forces with the signs, which are now linked together to form a *continuum*. Alexandre Cirici has commented: "The salient feature of Miró's work at this period is the development of an aspect which has always been present in it but which until this moment had remained of secondary importance: the use of calligraphy" (6).

The violence and the pronounced aggressiveness are parallel to that revealed in Picasso's work at that time through the exaggeration of the erotic element. Are we dealing with two different manifestations of the fight against time? In Picasso's case this combat originated in the need to maximise his vitality, which on another level struggles with the almost blinding light of reason that guided this artist. In Miró this struggle is channelled along *magic* paths, which take on the signs of the *enemy* in order to neutralise him. Like the child who imagines himself to be a ghost in order to overcome his fear of ghosts, Miró fights against time by adopting black and transforming it into a violent cry for life. We are dealing with a spell, which is also a synthesis that overcomes a dialectic stated by the simple fact of living.

Typical of Miró are the will to transgress, poetry, violence. Because of its characteristics and its purpose, the poster offers the artist the possibility of maximising the potential of these leanings. If Miró's painting, as Ragnar Hoppe expressed it, bursts like a shell against the wall of the Museum, the poster, from the moment of its conception, potentially carries within it this action, applied to the walls of the public highways. It is exactly this that constitutes the first quality required in a poster. But we already know that this intention is found at the root of all his production, as he himself, moreover, has made explicit on several occasions. We must remember that he once stated: "More than anything else, it is the visual impact that matters. Later the desire is felt to know what it says, what it represents. But only later" (7). It was to be expected, then, that this interest in surprise and impact should be exploited. In this respect, the poster summarises better than other works this aspiration of Miró's. The use of black emphasises this force so that the poster does not go unnoticed.

The Miró of the last few years is the most rebellious. Even though fantasy may frequently return, what seems to be the common denominator of the present period is the desire to *arouse* us. The posters, for example, do not try to attract us and entrance us, but to knock us down. There is a constant breaking-off and the forms tend to be unstable. In principle (because this is how it seems to be posed) they *ought* to rest on a base, with the support of *feet,* or on a border or several parallel strips constituting a *bed.* But Miró likes turning everything upside down, and we can no longer be sure of anything in this respect. Vertically rising forms are scarce, unlike the revolving forms and those *passing through,* moving around the bounded space of the poster. And all of this is not only a response to his will, but also to an inclination of his spirit.

This distortion and instability of the forms causes them to open up. We could understand black to be an originally compact mass or, on the other hand, an intrusive agent trying to invade the whole space. Dynamism, which is really fundamental, upsets the forms, distorting them. The edges fray. And then a kind of *mad rush* is produced: if there is no strong circular or marked transverse movement, the forms fly off in several directions, as if at the instigation of some centrifugal force. It is logical, in these circumstances, that there should be no main theme or minor secondary elements in their own right. That is to say, these differences occur with reference to size, but there is a noticeable absence of hierarchy, which, in Dupin's words, "is one of the principles of the marvellous and the fantastic in Miró's work" (8). These *minor* elements arise out of the explosion of that *cosmic egg* and, as always happens, they prove decisive to the interpretation of the whole. The body is thus womb and mother, from which, by means of a supposedly painful tearing-away, these ramifications emerge in the same way as the relatively independent symbols. We already know of the star, the dots, lines, rows of dots (which at times act as a border), spots, finger-prints or whole hand-prints, in the same way as those appendages that on occasions grow and multiply to the extent of appearing in *the theme*.

We find ourselves in a graphic world that has also to transmit certain information to us, with that impact which Miró always seeks. The splashes, whittled down, may be transformed into letters and numbers: those that form the message of the poster. But these names and figures may be entirely produced or finished off by typography. There are many possibilities, one of which is that the letters making up his signature are transformed into what the poster essentially has to say. Thus we see, clearly merged, the two aspects that may be presented by a poster made by an artist: the announcement of what the poster immediately refers to and that of the artist's own work, even though this may be involuntary. The poster that bids us go to this or that exhibition, or informs us of some congress, is also a Miró, and as such should be immediately recognised.

Keys to a language to mystify us

Miró's language, like Einstein's universe, is one of curves. The world is born out of the growth of a nucleus that expands in a space which, although limitless, is finite. Form is closely related to space: it is born for its use, conditioned by it and existing for it. But, at the same time (and we are already aware of this great artist's rebelliousness), the forms struggle to broaden the space, which is impossible because of the limitations implicit in the poster itself. Perhaps that is why they seem to curl up, swirl round and concentrate their strength, adding to the effect of the impact. Conscious of this spatial limitation, the theme emerges in the centre, although, carried along by its impulse, it then tends to fill it all. Because of the black strokes and the predominant role played by colour in Miró's work, the theme always stands out against the background, spattered with stains and dots like cosmic dust.

The alphabet of this curviform world is made up of polyphonic symbols which do not set out to give us keys to the meaning but rather *to mystify us*. As Marcelin Pleynet notes with great clarity, from Miró's first works up to the most recent ones, "he appears persistently to abandon all those who pretend to know what modern art is about, leaving them helpless". And all this is because "that which a rational approach to Miró's work perceives as a contradiction is within the unity that constitutes (only in so far as it is constituted as a unity) one of the keys to the meaning of this work" (9).

It must be remembered that the forms have their origin in the figure: Miró has rarely been exactly abstract, in the sense of turning his back on forms originating in the real world. It is just that these figures have undergone many transformations. Although not exactly human, neither do they cease to be so. In fact it could be said that above all they are so: that however distorted and ambiguous they may appear, they allude to man. They are a gentle caricature, a satire and a true likeness. But at the same time this human image — which is ultimately art's greatest theme, and cannot help being a mirror — opens up to admit a great many other *representations*. Miró's figures mean transformation. They are first one thing, step or process, then another. As believed by the orientals, whom Miró finds so interesting (Raymond Queneau has referred to the connection he thinks he can discern between Miró's language and Chinese script), more than the existence of things there is the existence of fluid relationships: it is wrong to give names and use nouns, we should rather make use of verbs, which provide us with the reality of the action.

Why should a man not also be an insect at the same time? Since Surrealism, and even long before that, this has seemed credible to us. Kafka, more than anyone, has presented it quite clearly in literature. The transformation, which is inevitable and has unsuspected results, reveals the metamorphosis of our *being*. And not only man and insect (which would amount to very little), the vegetable and animal worlds, but also the mineral world, which is just as alive, are present in Miró's universe. Moreover, these beings are not independent of each other: they appear united, strung together, by the *film* of their constant metamorphosis. There is but one form and it does not end in the furthest points of its ramifications, nor in the islands formed by the elements which have broken loose. For this reason we find it more *normal* to see an eye in a cluster, even though it may appear to be isolated. The same thing happens with heads, and with stars. Everything is the *same* in Miró's world, and there are no hierarchies, this we must remember. Carlos Castaneda, lying on the floor face to face with a beetle — in an encounter which fuses and identifies it with him — discovers that same truth to which Miró gives prominences in his posters. Human beings or animals, plants or crystalline transfigurations of matter, all these forms from Miró's world defy any linear classification, because they are the fruit of an imagination that allows us to discover, better than with the naked eye or a scientific instrument (which we know finds only its own reflected image), what nature *may be:* his own version of it, as approximate as any other, credible and valid.

Sign and colour

Colour is firstly the festive and lyrical element that characterises his work until 1960. Bright colours, which may be set off by strokes of black, or which on the other hand may surround a black stain, as happens, at the same time, in one and the same poster: the one for the International Surrealist Exhibition in 1947. We shall see that black is always there, although in the first posters it is rated as just one more colour without succeeding in constituting the dark *soul* of the work. On the other hand, as can be seen in the posters for the exhibitions at Maeght in 1947 and for the *ceramic* exhibition that he shared with Artigas in 1956, black contributes to the visual revelry that Miró's work still is today, adding a counterpoint only on the level of colour.

Colour must be referred to in relation to the composition and the form, since all three form part of a structure as strong as it is slack. This structure is moved and shaken, with greater or lesser force, by rhythm. The letters and the *minor* elements sway, as does also the whole, bending the axis-lines — as in the poster for the Maeght exhibition in 1953 — or making in flutter with the lightness of a handkerchief. This dynamism in some way breaks the even notion of the pictorial space, the notion presented in the poster. This also happens to a different extent in his contemporary pictures. Miró has always wanted to violate the rules. We must remember that in the early thirties aggessiveness — which has alternated with lyricism when they have not set up a conflict in the same work — presented itself by means of the thick black strokes which, at times in the shape of an angle or a cross, at others bending with the taut rigidity of metal (reminiscent of González's sculpture, perhaps?), filled the space. The forms at the beginning of the thirties consisted conceptually of one *single* one, which stretched out and disintegrated at the furthest edges. This fragmentation tendency reaches its peak in the *Constellations* series (1940-1941): as if in the firmament or suspended in a liquid, the tiny forms and the signs produced by the explosion fill the whole, take it over and *inhabit* it. However, they are not completely scattered or totally independent of each other, but rather strung together as if with a fine thread. Without this duality necessarily being established, another path leads to the unfolding and confrontation of two characters, or the emergence of several. They are the indefinable beings, but with distant or close kinship with man, to which I have already referred.

In the colourist period as well as in the period when he alternates black with vivid colours, Miró has been characterised by certain plastic colours which, being the most common, have acquired their own special significance at Miró's hands: they are *Miró* colours. This comes about because of the way in which he applies them in relation to certain definite forms, which are also very elementary. As Cirici has written: "the fact that Miró uses a range of colours that, at first sight and on enumerating them, seem to be what a European would classify as elementary, but which belong to an exotic register because of the functioning of their relationships, makes us realise that the articulations in Miró's painting are radically different from those in any work with a typical western register" (10).

The search for what is primordial and nuclear makes us associate it in some respects with what is archaic and primitive, in the same way as it can be associated with the *naïf:* this question of ingenuousness is one which, as Pleynet points out, no critic of Miró ever fails to run up against in one way or another, and which will elude his understanding if he approaches it in terms of reason alone (11). The conscious, patient and, to some extent, cold method with which Miró works, completes the task of the true prophet who contemplates unswervingly, with *nothing* to block his view, what he has before him. In an unsuspected way, this vision throws into relief, and gives value to, any apparently insignificant being or object. An old chair like those he has in his studio acquires, as for Van Gogh, an intensely thrilling existence. And this is what also happens on the plastic plane: at first the colours all had the same value; now, as a result of a *fall* in the world, the differences between *good* and *evil* arise: the related colours of life on the one hand and, on the other, black, the negation of colour and, symbolically, of life.

The forms of the first posters produced after the two wars (the Spanish Civil War and the Second World War) correspond to this pattern. In the field of the poster, leaving aside the 1919 project, the most typical works of Miró's happy magical period are those produced between 1947 and 1956. The next one, for the exhibition at the Galerie Matarasso in Nice in 1957, already displays something different: black, though not succeeding in dominating the other colours, takes on a new role, and the relaxation of form is given a different emphasis: it brings together certain plastic problems — those which were expressed in tachisme and non-figurative art — that find a personal frame-work in the subsequent period of development in Miró's work.

With the interval of the posters he produces between 1958 and 1960, 1961 is the year that the new style in posters appears, with the predominance of black and the dramatic character of the whole. The non-formal element is present not only in the vagueness of the limit and outlines, but also in the stains which spatter the background. The colour, in the strict sense, is nevertheless violent: it must be, in order to exist. Reds, blues, yellows and greens appear with violence and form, all together, the opposite pole of this chromatic dialogue-opposition. The power of black is revealed in the fact that it is responsible for the shaping of the principal signs. The black masses occupy extensive areas and threaten the rest, even to the point of invading other colours. This black is compact, but its very extension makes it less dense at times, creating a more transparent effect.

With time, and when this non-formal phase is over, the outline of the sign becomes more exact, and the other colours acquire autonomy. A certain *entente* seems to have been reached. One might say that black retains its role of creating the signs to communicate the poster's message, together with the principal nucleus of the plastic theme, and that the colours provide the real chromatic likeness, which is not exactly incidental, but rather a dialectic interplay. Obviously, black continues to have a visible preponderance: by reason of its very presence it carries more *weight,* but the objects seem to be clear and, with time, even the *colours* manage to prevail over black on the odd occasion, giving back that absolute, unalloyed happiness that defined the artist's earlier periods. With the new value given to black, every kind of being (or rather, one sole kind, under various forms) from his former periods disappears or becomes extraordinarily diagrammatic. Miró's mythology changes radically around 1960. Joan Teixidor is of the opinion that "it is not that the usual mythology disappears — the woman and the star, the tree and the sex, the sun and the moon — but they lose that amazing concrete solidity that belongs to his most elaborately produced work and become mere indicative symbols". And, as the president of the Fundació Miró goes on to say, "the graphic quality has become more forceful and explosive and does not need to resort to reiterations. The spot bursts out as if to empty itself and the line that cleaves and cracks it is no more than a gesture. The same mechanical procedure facilitates these unexpected explosions..." (12). On occasions, the form outlined in black now gives shape to certain *beings* which retain an element of connection. They are not

18

exactly *insignificant,* or marvellous as such, but they are, rather, other different beings, magnified by the black and of an aggressive nature. But the notes of vivid colour and the context in which they occur — Miró's world — help us to understand that they are basically the same beings, which have been intimately divided by a certain light: if those from previous decades were innocent and could not do us good or ill, and for this reason amazed us (ecstasy was what they set out to provoke), those of today are *stained* with humanity, and as such are *ambiguous* and embody a *danger*. Basically, and in contrast to the others, they present a conflict which expects no solution, only *consciousness*. As always happens, it is necessary to be able to read the minor elements, the apparently insignificant graphic qualities, all that which remains, or so it seems, outside the main flow. In their very spontaneity, all these elements prove to be enlightening: they illuminate the meaning of the main theme and open it up for us to understand. For this main theme closes on itself, heightens the meaning, cuts off the bridges. The *accessory* elements are loose ends for us to hold on to, because it is they that must lead us with greater ease to the heart of the main theme. Being inaccessible gives this main theme an element of self-sufficiency; but we can pick up certain flourishes from the spaces around it which hold the over-all meaning.

There is one form typical of Miró which has acquired great importance in the posters: the one which ressembles an eye and which usually appears in clusters (as in the wings of a few Romanesque angels). Sometimes it is round, but more often it is almond-shaped. It may, however, also be reminiscent of the female sexual organ. In the shape of an almond it may also suggest other meanings to us, and the one referring to its possible mystical character only serves to emphasise, almost brutally, the other. At all events, it is an opening. Within the initially compact space of the poster, by virtue of its clenched-fist character that rushes out towards the spectator, it opens the space to the meaning in the main theme that wishes to conceal itself from us (thus compelling us to make a journey).

The colour, throughout the period beginning in 1960, can be seen very much surrounded by black, which encloses it in the forms it creates or in strokes and spots applied with precision. The composition itself and the forms give shape to certain compartments which the colour fills in. The two basic Miró colours are red and blue, and on the framework of this basic duality appear the other colours. Yellow and green are those likely to impart the note of jollity and create the sources that distract us from the essential conflict, which continues to be the opposition of black to colour, where the presence of red and blue does not introduce any basic variations: they continue to be *serious* key colours. Yellow and green on the plane of colour follow the role attributed to the *minor* elements on the level of composition and form. Yellow and green speak to us of the colours' *soul* that underlies the contemporary theatrical quality, and the path of his posters must be followed assiduously in order to see how that marginal colour appears, or at times bursts forth, as if unnoticed (this may more easily occur in posters for *minor* exhibitions: not for their intrinsic importance but because of the comparison with the great anthological exhibitions). Thus we find the gay and colourfully uninhibited poster for the exhibition at the Galería Theo in Madrid in 1978, with black playing an unassuming role, in contrast to the two posters for the contemporary exhibitions also held in Madrid: the painting exhibition and the exhibition of graphic work organised by the Dirección General del Patrimonio Artístico, Archivos y Museos del Ministerio español de Cultura.

Red and yellow, still within Miró's range, appear in the Catalan flag, which we find in several posters. It must be remembered that in the first poster, the one planned for the magazine *L'Instant*, this flag could already be seen, waving to the uneven rhythm of a cubism in its critical, futurist variation. It then appears, also fully justified, whenever appropriate to the theme: posters for the *Primer de Maig 1968, II Congreso Jurídico Catalán* (1971), *Per un teatre a Catalunya* (1973), *Futbol Club Barcelona, 75 Aniversari* (1974) and *Congrés de Cultura Catalana* (1977).

Requests and preferences

The flag theme introduces us to the different types of posters which could emerge, not only with reference to their themes, but also as a result of the kinds of proposals or circumstances that were present in the origin of the posters themselves, public or private motives or the countries where they were published. It should be borne in mind that to a certain extent there is always a fortuitous element in the motives, especially at the beginning, when there is little activity in this area. But, whatever the reason, it is significant that the first poster (though no more than a preparatory design, as we already know) should be for a Catalan magazine, and the second one for the Spanish Republic Pavilion at the Paris International Exhibition in 1937. Basically, all these posters are greatly indicative of Miró's leanings and his over-all artistic activity. Even contingency, whether real or apparent, is also usually significant. Logically, most of his posters refer to his own exhibitions, largely organised by Maeght or important museums. It all has its explanation in the development of Miró's work and of the personality of the man himself. And for this reason we must not leave out the tributes: the most moving ones dedicated to Catalonia and, on a personal level, to his friends Joan Prats, Sert and Artigas. Miró's activity in the field of the poster has progressively increased, owing to the constant increase in his prestige and also to the importance Miró has succeeded in achieving for Catalonia, as a symbol of freedom in the last stages of the Francoist era and as one of the pillars of national identity. This concern reaches its peak with the poster produced in support of the Statute of Catalan Autonomy, which could not be published.

The poster, a perishable and lasting art

Miró and his work constitute a key factor in the knowledge of the new collective image throughout the world. The influence he has had on the new generations of artists, and also on interior design, graphic design and other fields, has been both vast and decisive. Within this influence the poster plays an important role, since it is, in fact, created in order to act directly upon the public. In the street, enlarged in some cases, the world of Miró is present in its entirety in those rectangular spaces, the formal association of which we find in the concept of a picture. But the poster, and more so in Miró's case, goes beyond those limits, and we can properly speak of a mural with all its social implications. Miró's poster, having fulfilled its purpose of making known something very specific, continues to interest us precisely because it is art.

There is a poster which does not appear in this book, because of its special characteristics and because it disappeared without trace, except for a few photographs: the one he painted on the glass walls of the Colegio de Arquitectos in Barcelona in 1969 to advertise his exhibition "Miró-the other", and which he himself then erased once the exhibition was over. I had occasion to follow at close range the whole process and controversy which its disappearance gave rise to. I do not know whether the significance of that action was generally understood. Every poster is born with this intention, and it is of secondary importance whether they may subsequently be kept: they are born to be ripped down, replaced or covered by others. Apart from the conditioning and peculiarities that the market imposes on contemporary plastic creation, a work of art is above all something to be enjoyed, not to be kept. It is, of course, natural and logical that it should be kept: culture operates by means of accumulation and transfusion and the work of any artist must be preserved because it may continue to be something alive for the future. But in the case of the poster that Miró painted and later erased himself, the fact that it disappeared constituted in itself an artistic action, the value of which was far greater than that of what we lost when it disappeared. Half-way between the ordinary poster and process art, which leaves no trace, this poster sums up an attitude which from beginning to end is one of rebellion and constant creation, for which destruction is necessary.

As an artistic event, the poster has no exchange value in general (although, as with everything, it could eventually have one if its rarity brought it about), it is not a *work*. But we, and very probably Miró, too, find it highly revitalising that something, in this respect, should have no worth. At the root of the poster is found his collective vocation along with his elusiveness. A poster sets out to synthesize with an image (more explicitly, we know, than ten thousand words) a plan or a reality that affects or may affect many people. It bears some resemblance to a flag, except that its waving is symbolic. On the wall, colours, with their rhythm and their graphic quality, always constitute the announcement of a good piece of artistic news, ever different though ever identical in its deep and very personal plastic truth.

NOTES

(1) F. Enel: *L'affiche: fonctions, langage, rhétorique.* Maison Mame 1971. Spanish edition: *El cartel: lenguaje, funciones, retórica.* Fernando Torres Editor, Valencia, 1974, page 68.

(2) Folder of 52 posters by various artists with a text by Jacques Prévert. Mourlot, éditeur et imprimeur, Paris, 1963.

(3) Three volumes have so far appeared, the Spanish edition of which has been undertaken by Ediciones Polígrafa, S.A., Barcelona.

(4) Attilio Rossi: *I manifesti.* Fratelli Fabbri Editori, Milan, 1966, pages 144-150.

(5) Giuseppe Marchiori: *Miró à travers son temps.* "XXe. siècle", Hommage à Joan Miró, Paris, 1972.

(6) Alexandre Cirici Pellicer: *Miró llegit.* Edicions 62, Barcelona, 1971. Spanish version: *Miró en su obra.* Editorial Labor, S.A., Barcelona, 1970, page 147.

(7) Pierre Schneider: *Les dialogues du Louvre.* Denoël édit., Paris, 1971. Quoted by Marcelin Pleynet: *Miró et la culture moderne.* "Derrière le Miroir", No. 231, Maeght Editeur, Paris, November 1978.

(8) Jacques Dupin: *Joan Miró: la vie et l'oejuvre.* Flammarion, Paris, 1961, page 472.

(9) Marcelin Pleynet: *Miró et la culture moderne.* "Derrière le Miroir", No. 231, Maeght éditeur, Paris, November 1978.

(10) Alexandre Cirici Pellicer: *op. cit.,* page 116.

(11) Marcelin Pleynet: *op. cit.*

(12) Joan Teixidor: *Miró lithographe III,* Maeght éditeur, Paris, 1977. Spanish version: *Miró litógrafo III.* Ediciones Polígrafa, S.A., Barcelona, 1978, page 19.

ILLUSTRATIONS

1. "AVIAT L'INSTANT". 1919.

Poster planned for the fortnightly magazine "L'Instant" (Barcelona-París).

Oil-painting on cardboard, 107 × 76 cm.

Joaquim Gomis Collection, Barcelona.

BIBLIOGRAPHY:

PERUCHO, Juan: *Joan Miró y Cataluña*. Ed. Polígrafa, S.A., Barcelona, 1968, page 25, No. 15.
Catalogue for the Exhibition "Miró Barcelona 1968-1969". Barcelona City Council, Antiguo Hospital de la Santa Cruz, Barcelona, 1968, page 58, No. 10, plate 5.

Catalogue for the Exhibition "Miró, l'œuvre graphique". Musée d'Art Moderne de la Ville de Paris, 1974, page 139, No. 530.

CIRICI, Alexandre: *Miró Mirall*. Ed. Polígrafa, S.A., Barcelona, 1977, page 18, No. 5. "La Vanguardia Española", Barcelona, 28 January 1978.

Catalogue for the Exhibition "Joan Miró. Obra Gráfica". Halls of the Dirección General del Patrimonio Artístico, Archivos y Museos, Madrid, 1978, page 81, No. 217.

2. "AIDEZ L'ESPAGNE". 1937.

Poster produced by Joan Miró in support of the Spanish Republican Government during the Civil War.

This poster was later used for the exhibition "Venice Biennale. Spain: avant-garde art and social reality, 1936-1976", held at the Fundació Joan Miró in Barcelona (December 1976-February 1977).

BIBLIOGRAPHY:

"Cahiers d'Art", Paris, 1937, Vol. XII, Nos. 4-5 (reproduction of the poster in *pochoir*).
SOBY, James Thrall: *Miró*. Museum of Modern Art, New York, 1959, page 91.
DUPIN, Jacques: *Miró*. Éd. Flammarion, Paris, 1961, page 289.
CIRICI, Alexandre: *Miró en su obra*. Ed. Labor, Barcelona, 1970, page 39.
DIEHL, Gaston: *Miró*. Éd. Flammarion, Paris, 1974, page 53.
HERRMANNS, Ralph: *Affischer av Miró*. A.H. Grafik, Stockholm, 1974, page 18, No. 1.
Several authors: *España. Vanguardia artística y realidad social: 1936-1976*. Ed. Gustavo Gili, Barcelona, 1976, cover.
"Triunfo", Madrid, year XXXI, No. 700, 26 June 1976, cover.
JOHANSSON, Kjell A.: *Miró en Escania*. "Dagens Nyheter", Stockholm, 30 June 1976.
PENROSE, Roland: *Miró*. Ed. Daimon, Barcelona, 1976, page 89.
"Le Nouvel Observateur", Paris, 9 August 1976, page 15.
CIRICI, Alexandre: *Miró Mirall*. Ed. Polígrafa, S.A., Barcelona, 1977, page 150, No. 166.
RAILLARD, Georges: *Joan Miró. Ceci est la couleur de mes rêves*. Ed. du Seuil, Paris, 1977. page 169.
"Avui", Barcelona, 20 April 1978.
AMÓN, Santiago: *Tres horas con Joan Miró*. "El País semanal", Madrid, 18 June 1978, page 16.
"Última Hora", Palma de Mallorca, September 1978. Special issue devoted to Joan Miró, page 58.

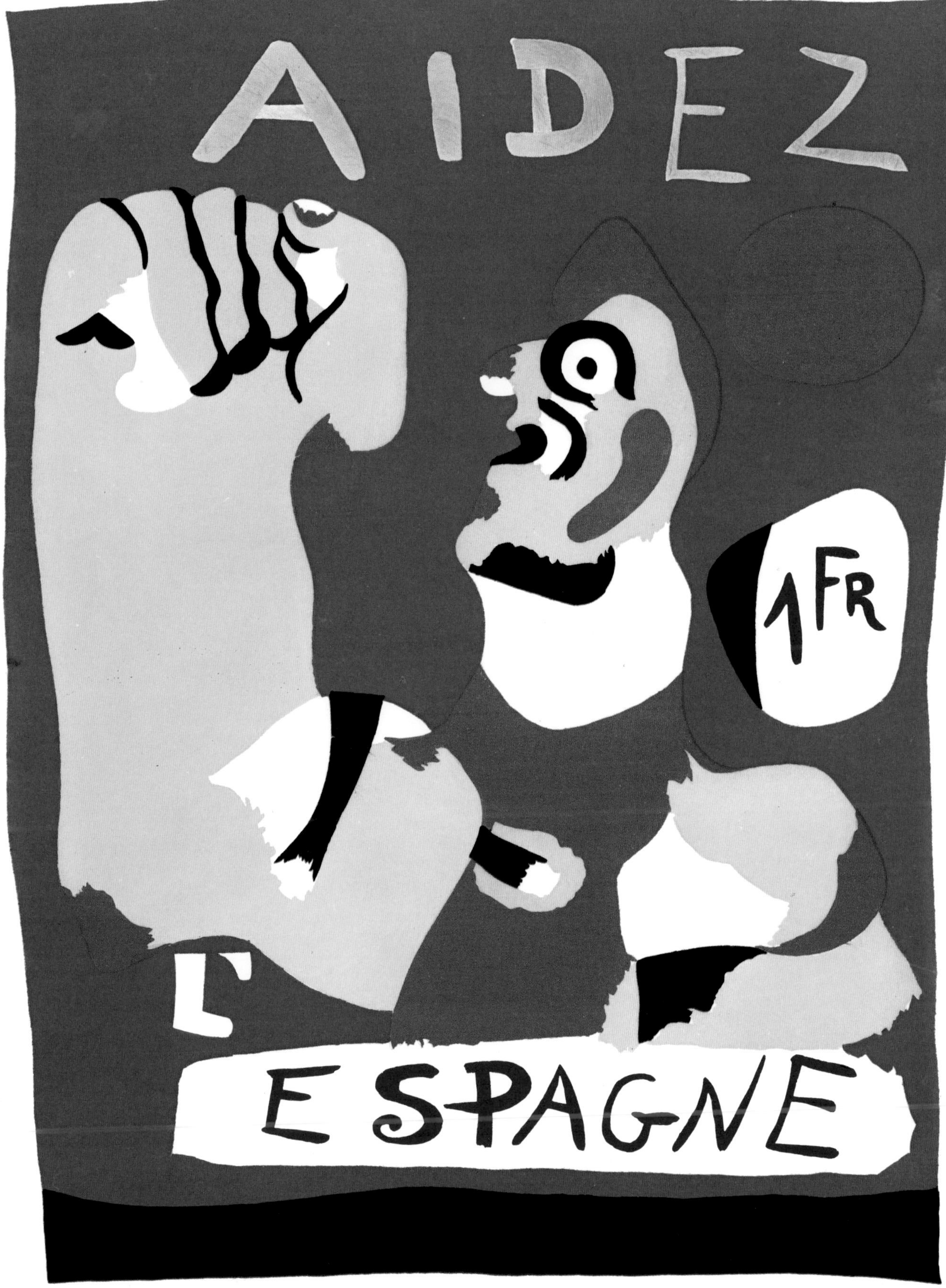
AIDEZ
1FR
L'
ESPAGNE

3. EXPOSITION INTERNATIONALE DU SURRÉALISME. 1947.

Poster produced by Joan Miró for the exhibition "Le Surréalisme", organised by the Galerie Maeght in Paris in 1947.

Publication:
500 copies on standard paper.
Size: 64.5 × 47 cm.
Some copies *avant la lettre* on Marais paper, signed on the original plate.
Printing process: colour lithographic press.
Size: 64.5 × 47 cm.

Publisher: Galerie Maeght, Paris.
Printer: Mourlot, Paris.

BIBLIOGRAPHY:

Catalogue for the Exhibition "Joan Miró. Das graphische Gesamtwerk". Kestner-Gesellschaft, Hanover, 1957, No. 177.

Catalogue for the Exhibition "Miró. Das graphische Werk". Kaiser Wilhelm Museum, Krefeld, 1957, No. 177.

MOURLOT, Fernand: *Les affiches originales des maîtres de l'École de Paris: Braque, Chagall, Dufy, Léger, Matisse, Miró, Picasso.* André Sauret Éd., Montecarlo, 1959, No. 48.

Catalogue for the Exhibition "Miró. Art graphique". Modern Art Museum, Tokyo, 1962, No. 227.

LEIRIS, Michel: *Joan Miró Litógrafo I.* Ed. Polígrafa, S.A., Barcelona, 1972, pages 106-107, No. 57.

HERRMANNS, Ralph: *Affischer av Miró.* A.H. Grafik, Stockholm, 1974, page 19, No. 2.

Catalogue for the Exhibition "Miró, l'œuvre graphique". Musée d'Art Moderne de la Ville de Paris, 1974, page 139, page 141, No. 531.

Catalogue for the Exhibition "Joan Miró. Obra Gráfica". Halls of the Dirección General del Patrimonio Artístico, Archivos y Museos, Madrid, pages 80-81, No. 218.

Catalogue for the Exhibition "Joan Miró. Grafica". Palazzo Pubblico, Siena, 1979, pages 71 and 90, No. 205.

XPOSITION
INTERNATIONALE DU
SURRÉALISME
1 9 4 7
GALERIE MAEGHT
13 RUE DE TÉHÉRAN PARIS

4. GALERIE MAEGHT EXHIBITION. 1948.

Poster for Miró's first individual exhibition at the Galerie Maeght, Paris, where he showed 88 works — painting and ceramics (November-December 1948).

Publication:
300 copies on Marais paper.
Size: 65 × 50 cm.

Some copies *avant la lettre* (without the lithographed Galerie Maeght text) on Marais paper, signed.
Size: 65 × 50 cm.

75 copies *avant la lettre,* on Rives paper, modified by Joan Miró, numbered and signed; lithograph called *Person and bird.* Printing process: colour lithographic press.
Size: 65 × 50 cm.
Publisher: Galerie Maeght, Paris.
Printer: Mourlot, Paris.

BIBLIOGRAPHY:

Catalogue for the Exhibition "Joan Miró. Das graphische Gesamtwerk". Kestner-Gesellschaft, Hanover, 1957, No. 178.
Catalogue for the Exhibition "Miró. Das graphische Werk". Kaiser Wilhelm Museum, Krefeld, 1957, No. 178.
WEMBER, Paul: *Joan Miró. Farbige Lithographien.* Insel-Verlag, Wiesbaden, 1959, No. 22.
MOURLOT, Fernand: *Les affiches originales des maîtres de l'École de Paris: Braque, Chagall, Dufy, Léger, Matisse, Miró, Picasso.* André Sauret Ed., Montecarlo, 1959, No. 49.
Catalogue for the Exhibition "Miró. Art graphique", Modern Art Museum, Tokyo, 1962, No. 228.
Catalogue "Derrière le Miroir et Affiches". Maeght Ed., Paris, 1971, page 21, No. 23.
LEIRIS, Michel: *Joan Miró Litógrafo I.* Ed. Polígrafa, S.A., Barcelona, 1972, pages 125-126, Nos. 67-68.
HERRMANNS, Ralph: *Affischer av Miró.* A.H. Grafik, Stockholm, 1974, page 22, No. 21.
Catalogue for the Exhibition "Miró, l'œuvre graphique". Musée d'Art Moderne de la Ville de Paris, 1974, page 139, No. 532.

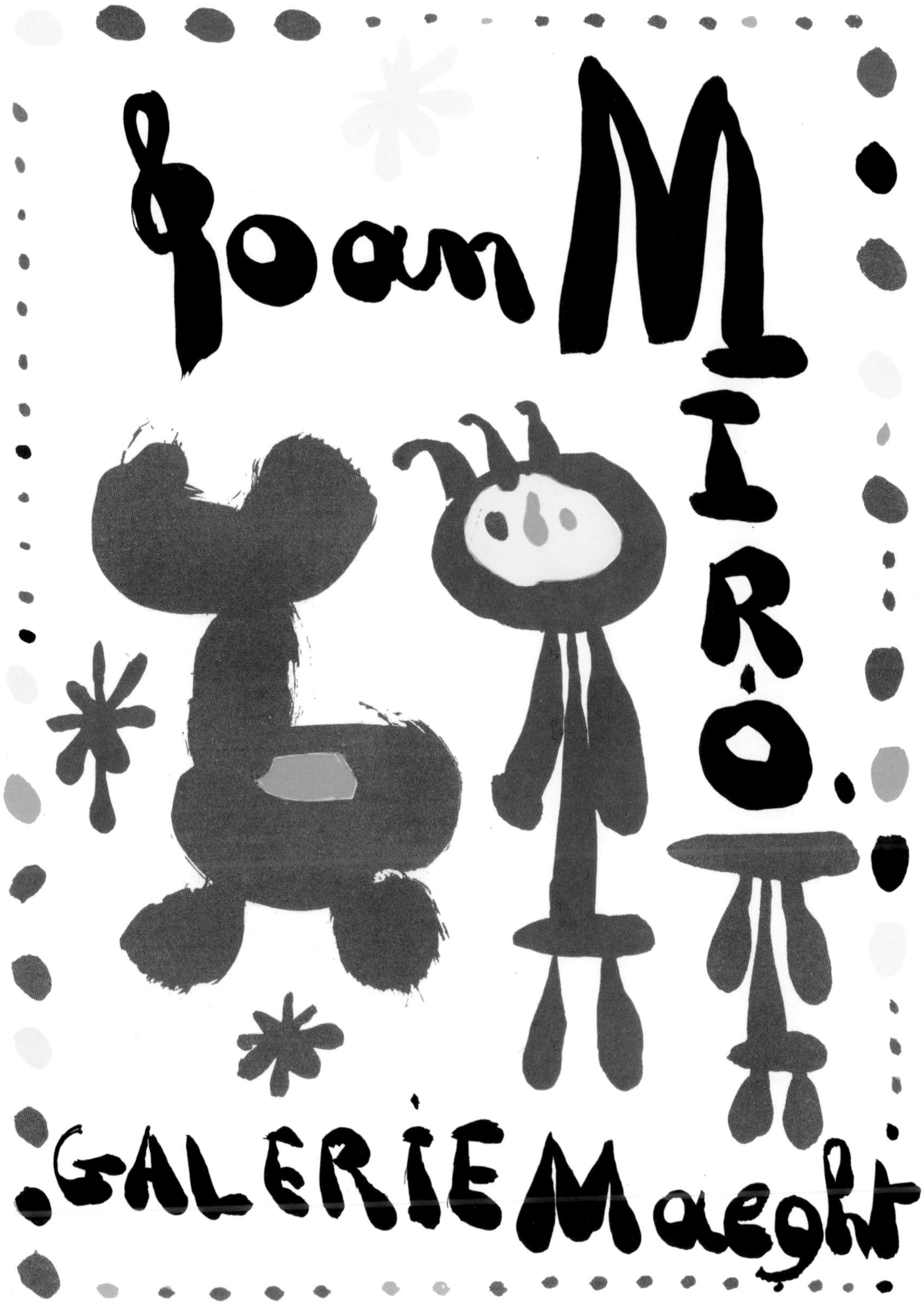
Joan Miró
GALERIE Maeght

5. "SCULPTURES - ART GRAPHIQUE" EXHIBITION. 1950.

Poster produced for the exhibition of 130 of Miró's works at the Galerie Maeght, Paris (May-June 1950).

Publication:
500 copies on standard paper.
Size: 64.5 × 48.5 cm.
There are reprints of this poster.
40 copies *avant la lettre,* without a lithographed text, on Arches paper, numbered and signed. This lithograph goes under the name of "Person and red sun I".

"Person and red sun II": *avant la lettre,* composition embellished by a large personal figure in black.

40 copies on Arches paper, numbered and signed.

"Person with stars": inversion of the black lithographic stone corresponding to the *avant la lettre* printing of the poster, the whole being reprocessed.

75 copies on Arches paper, numbered and signed.

Printing process: colour lithographic press.
Size: 65 × 50 cm.

Publisher: Galerie Maeght, Paris.

Printer: Mourlot, Paris.

BIBLIOGRAPHY:

Catalogue for the Exhibition "Miró. Das graphische Werk". Kaiser Wilhelm Museum, Krefeld, 1957, Nos. 99-100-101-179.
Catalogue for the Exhibition "Joan Miró. Das graphische Gesamtwerk". Kestner-Gesellschaft, Hanover, 1957, No. 179.
MOURLOT, Fernand: *Les affiches originales des maîtres de l'École de Paris: Braque, Chagall, Dufy, Léger, Matisse, Miró, Picasso.* Andrés Sauret Ed., Montecarlo, 1959, No. 50.
WEMBER, Paul: *Joan Miró. Farbige Lithographien.* Insel-Verlag, Wiesbaden, 1959, Nos. 2-3-4.
Catalogue for the Exhibition "Miró. Art graphique". Modern Art Museum, Tokyo, 1962, No. 229.
Catalogue "Derrière le Miroir et Affiches". Maeght Ed., Paris, 1971, page 32.
LEIRIS, Michel: *Joan Miró Litógrafo I.* Ed. Polígrafa, S.A., Barcelona, 1972, pages 164-168, Nos. 92-95.
HERRMANNS, Ralph: *Affischer av Miró.* A.H. Grafik, Stockholm, 1974, page 23, No. 4.
Catalogue for the Exhibition "Miró l'œuvre graphique". Musée d'Art Moderne de la Ville de Paris, 1974, page 139, No. 533.
Catalogue for the Exhibition "Joan Miró. Grafica". Palazzo Pubblico, Siena, 1979, page 90, No. 206.

Galerie MAEGHT

MIRÓ

ART

Sculptures

Graphi

6. "ŒUVRES RÉCENTES" EXHIBITION. 1953.

Poster for the exhibition of Miró's painting and graphic work at the Galerie Maeght, Paris (June-August 1953).

Publication:
350 copies on standard paper.
Size: 67.5 × 51 cm.

150 copies *avant la lettre* on Arches paper numbered and signed. Printing process: colour lithographic press.
Size: 75.5 × 55.5 cm.

Publisher: Galerie Maeght, Paris.
Printer: Mourlot, Paris.

BIBLIOGRAPHY:

Catalogue for the Exhibition "Joan Miró. Das graphische Gesamtwerk". Kestner-Gesellschaft, Hanover, 1957, No. 180.
Catalogue for the Exhibition "Miró. Das graphische Werk". Kaiser Wilhelm Museum, Krefeld, 1957, No. 180.
MOURLOT, Fernand: *Les affiches originales des maîtres de l'École de Paris: Braque, Chagall, Dufy, Léger, Matisse, Miró, Picasso*. André Sauret Ed., Montecarlo, 1959, No. 51.
Catalogue for the Exhibition "Miró. Art graphique". Modern Art Museum, Tokyo, 1962, No. 230.
Catalogue "Derrière le Miroir et Affiches". Maeght Ed., Paris, 1971, page 51, No. 25.
HERRMANNS, Ralph: *Affischer av Miró*. A.H. Grafik, Stockholm, 1974, page 65, No. 25.
Catalogue for the Exhibition "Miró, l'œuvre graphique". Musée d'Art Moderne de la Ville de Paris, 1974, page 139, No. 534.
QUENEAU, Raymond: *Joan Miró Litógrafo II*. Ed. Polígrafa, S.A., Barcelona, 1975, pages 42-43, No. 123.
Catalogue for the Exhibition "Joan Miró. Grafica". Palazzo Pubblico, Siena, 1979, page 90, No. 207.

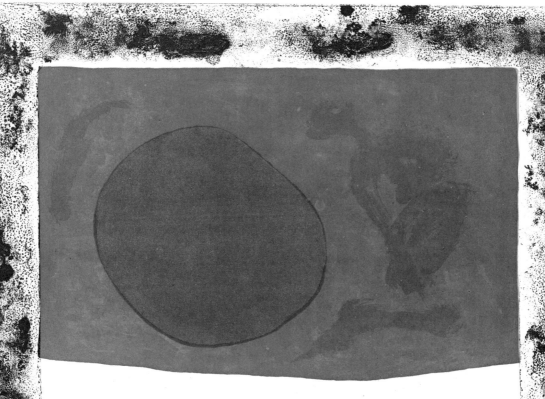

Galerie   Maeght

œuvres récentes

7. "TERRES DE GRAND FEU" EXHIBITION. 1956

Poster produced for the exhibition of 43 ceramic pieces, made by Miró and Llorens Artigas between 1950 and 1956, at the Galerie Maeght, Paris (June-July 1956).

Publication:
500 copies on standard paper.
Size: 75 × 52.5 cm.

200 copies *avant la lettre* on Arches paper, numbered and signed.
Printing process: colour lithographic press.
Size: 75 × 52.5 cm.

Publisher: Galerie Maeght, Paris
Printer: Mourlot, Paris.

BIBLIOGRAPHY:

Catalogue for the Exhibition "Miró. Das graphische Werk". Kaiser Wilhelm Museum, Krefeld, 1957, No. 181.

Catalogue for the Exhibition "Joan Miró. Das graphische Gesamtwerk". Kestner-Gesellschaft, Hanover, 1957, No. 181.

MOURLOT, Fernand: *Les affiches originales des maîtres de l'École de Paris: Braque, Chagall, Dufy, Léger, Matisse, Miró, Picasso*. André Sauret Éd., Montecarlo, 1959, No. 53.

Catalogue for the Exhibition "Miro. Art graphique". Modern Art Museum, Tokyo, 1962, No. 232.

Catalogue for the Exhibition "Miró Barcelona 1968-1969". Barcelona City Council, antiguo Hospital de la Santa Cruz, Barcelona, 1968, page 84, No. 377.

Catalogue "Derrière le Miroir et Affiches". Maeght Ed., Paris, 1971, page 65.

HERRMANNS, Ralph: *Affischer av Miró*. A.H. Grafik, Stockholm, 1974, page 65, No. 27.

Catalogue for the Exhibition "Miró, l'œuvre graphique". Musée d'Art Moderne de la Ville de Paris, 1974, page 139, No. 535.

QUENEAU, Raymond: *Joan Miró Litógrafo II*. Ed. Polígrafa, S.A., Barcelona, 1975, page 73, No. 152.

Catalogue for the Exhibition "Joan Miró. Obra Gráfica". Halls of the Dirección General del Patrimonio Artístico, Archivos y Museos, Madrid, 1978, page 91, No. 219.

Catalogue for the Exhibition "Joan Miró. Grafica". Palazzo Pubblico, Siena, 1979, page 90, No. 208.

8. "MIRÓ: PEINTURES, LITHOGRAPHIES, SCULPTURES, CÉRAMIQUES" EXHIBITION. 1957

Poster produced for the exhibition of Miró's paintings, lithographs, sculptures and ceramics in the Galerie Matarasso, Nice (17 May to 17 June 1957).

Publication:
500 copies on standard paper.
Size: 67 × 49 cm.

125 copies *avant la lettre,* without the lithographed name of Miró, on Arches paper, numbered and signed.

Printing process: colour lithographic press.
Size: 56.5 × 43.5 cm.

Publisher: Galerie Matarasso, Nice.
Printer: Mourlot, Paris.

BIBLIOGRAPHY:

MOURLOT, Fernand: *Les affiches originales des maîtres de l'École de Paris: Braque, Chagall, Dufy, Léger, Matisse, Miró, Picasso.* André Sauret Éd., Montecarlo, 1959, No. 54.
HERRMANNS, Ralph: *Affischer av Miró.* A.H. Grafik, Stockholm, 1974, page 26, No. 5.
Catalogue for the Exhibition "Miró, l'œuvre graphique". Musée d'Art Moderne de la Ville de Paris, 1974, page 139, No. 536.
QUENEAU, Raymond: *Joan Miró Litógrafo II.* Ed. Polígrafa, S.A., Barcelona, 1975, page 101, No. 177 and page 103, No. 179.

PEINTURES   SCULPTURES

LITHOGRAPHIES   CÉRAMIQUES

GALERIE MATARASSO 36 "B" DUBOUCHAGE NICE

DU 17 MAI AU 17 JUIN 1957

9. "À TOUTE ÉPREUVE" EXHIBITION. 1958

Poster produced for the presentation at Berggruen & Cie., Paris of the book *À toute épreuve* with 77 wood engravings by Joan Miró, published by Gérald Cramer, Geneva (25 April to 17 May 1958).

This poster was used for the presentation of this book in the Galerie Gérald Cramer, Geneva, from 18 December 1958 to 30 January 1959.

Publication:
800 copies on Rives paper for Berggruen & Cie.
500 copies on Rives paper for Galerie Gérald Cramer.
Size: 52 × 38 cm.

125 copies *avant la lettre* on Rives paper, numbered and signed.
Printing process: colour xylography.
Size: 52 × 37 cm.

Publisher: Gérald Cramer, Geneva.
Printer: Féqquet et Baudier, Paris (for the poster).
        Lacourière, Paris (for the woodcut *avant la lettre*).

BIBLIOGRAPHY:

Catalogue for the Exhibition "À toute épreuve". Galerie Berggruen, Paris, 1958.
MOURLOT, Fernand: *Les affiches originales des maîtres de l'École de Paris: Braque, Chagall, Dufy, Léger, Matisse, Miró, Picasso.* André Sauret Éd., Montecarlo, 1959, No. 55.
HERRMANNS, Ralph: *Affischer av Miró.* A.H. Grafik, Stockholm, 1974, page 27, No. 6.

JOAN MIRÓ

bois gravés pour

A TOUTE ÉPREUVE de PAUL ELUARD

EXPOSITION

GALERIE CRAMER

du 18 décembre 1958 au 30 janvier 1959   13, rue de Chantepoulet, Genève

10. "JOAN MIRÓ: CONSTELLATIONS" EXHIBITION. 1959.

Poster produced for the presentation at Berggruen & Cie., Paris of the book *Constellations* published in New York by Pierre Matisse, with text by André Breton and facsimile reproduction of the series of water colours *Constellations* by Miró.

Publication:
900 copies on standard paper.
Size: 68 × 49 cm.
150 copies *avant la lettre* on Arches paper, numbered and signed.

Printing process: colour lithographic press.
Size: 65 × 49 cm.

Publisher: Berggruen & Cie., Paris.
Printer: Mourlot, Paris.

BIBLIOGRAPHY:

MOURLOT, Fernand: *Les affiches originales des maîtres de l'École de Paris: Braque, Chagall, Dufy, Léger, Matisse, Miró, Picasso*. André Sauret Éd., Montecarlo, 1959, No. 100.
TAILLANDIER, Ivon: *Mirografías*. Ed. Gustavo Gili, S.A., Barcelona, 1972, page 183.
HERRMANNS, Ralph: *Affischer av Miró*. A.H. Grafik, Stockholm, 1974, page 30, No. 7.
Catalogue for the Exhibition "Miró, l'œuvre graphique". Musée d'Art Moderne de la Ville de Paris, 1974, page 139, No. 537.
QUENEAU, Raymond: *Joan Miró Litógrafo II*. Ed. Polígrafa, S.A., Barcelona, 1975, page 119, No. 191.
Catalogue for the Exhibition "Joan Miró. Obra Gráfica". Halls of the Dirección General del Patrimonio Artístico, Archivos y Museos, Madrid, 1978, page 81, No. 220.
Catalogue for the Exhibition "Joan Miró. Grafica". Palazzo Pubblico, Siena, 1979, page 90, No. 209.

JOAN MIRÓ
Constellations
PIERRE MATISSE ÉDITEUR

EXPOSITION CHEZ
BERGGRUEN - 70 RUE DE L'UNIVERSITÉ - PARIS

MOURLOT. IMP., PARIS

11. "POÈTES, SCULPTEURS, PEINTRES" EXHIBITION. 1960.

Poster produced by Miró for the collective exhibition *Poètes, Sculpteurs, Peintres,* held at the Galerie Maeght, Paris (June-September 1960).

This lithograph, embellished and modified by Miró, was used as illustration No. 17 in the book *Album 19* (1961).

Publication:
500 copies on standard paper.
200 copies on Rives paper.

Printing process: colour lithographic press.
Size: 68.5 × 44.5 cm.

Publisher: Galerie Maeght, Paris.
Printer: Arte Adrien Maeght, Paris.

BIBLIOGRAPHY:

Catalogue for the Exhibition "Miró. Art graphique". Modern Art Museum, Tokyo, 1962, No. 233.
Catalogue for the Exhibition "Miró Barcelona 1968-1969". Barcelona City Council, Antiguo Hospital de la Santa Cruz, Barcelona, 1968, page 84, No. 378.
Catalogue "Derrière le Miroir et Affiches". Maeght Éd., Paris, 1971, page 85, No. 70.
HERRMANNS, Ralph: *Affischer av Miró*. A.H. Grafik, Stockholm, 1974, page 65, No. 28.
Catalogue for the Exhibition "Miró, l'œuvre graphique". Musée d'Art Moderne de la Ville de Paris, 1974, page 139, No. 538.
QUENEAU, Raymond: *Joan Miró Litógrafo II*. Ed. Polígrafa, S.A., Barcelona, 1975, page 126, No. 196.
Catalogue for the Exhibition "Joan Miró. Grafica". Palazzo Pubblico, Siena, 1979, page 90, No. 210.

POÈTES
SCULPTEURS
PEINTRES

GALERIE MAEGHT

© Editeur MAEGHT Imprimeur

12. "MIRÓ - MUSÉE DE L'ATHÉNÉE". 1961.

Poster produced for the Exhibition "OEuvre graphique, céramiques", at the Musée de l'Athénée, Geneva (10 June to 14 July 1961).

Publication:
Indefinite number of copies on standard paper.

Size: 64 × 44 cm.

100 copies *avant la lettre* on Rives paper, numbered and signed.
Printing process: colour lithographic press.
Size: 75 × 55 cm.

Publisher: Edwin Engelberts, Paris.
Printer: Arte Adrien Maeght, Paris.

BIBLIOGRAPHY:

HERRMANS, Ralph: *Affischer av Miró*. A.H. Grafik, Stockholm, 1974, page 31, No. 8.
Catalogue for the Exhibition "Miro, l'œuvre graphique". Musée d'Art Moderne de la Ville de Paris, 1974, page 140, No. 539.
QUENEAU, Raymond: *Joan Miró Litógrafo II*. Ed. Polígrafa, S.A., Barcelona, 1975, page 206, No. 264.

13. "PEINTURES MURALES" EXHIBITION. 1961.

Poster produced for the presentation of six mural paintings by Joan Miró at the Galerie Maeght, Paris (23 June to 31 July 1961).

Publication:
Indefinite number of copies on standard paper.
Size: 67 × 48.5 cm.

100 copies *avant la lettre,* on Rives paper, numbered and signed.
Printing process: colour lithographic press.
Size: 67 × 48.5 cm.

Publisher: Galerie Maeght, Paris.
Printer: Arte Adrien Maeght, Paris.

BIBLIOGRAPHY:

Catalogue for the Exhibition "Miró. Art graphique". Modern Art Museum, Tokyo, 1962, No. 235.
Catalogue "Derrière le Miroir et Affiches". Maeght Ed., Paris, 1971, page 92.
TAILLANDIER, Yvon: *Mirografías.* Ed. Gustavo Gili, S.A., Barcelona, 1972, page 186.
HERRMANNS, Ralph: *Affischer av Miró.* A.H. Grafik, Stockholm, 1974, page 65, No. 30.
Catalogue for the Exhibition "Miró, l'œuvre graphique". Musée d'Art Moderne de la Ville de Paris, 1974, page 140, No. 540.
QUENEAU, Raymond: *Joan Miró Litógrafo II.* Ed. Polígrafa, S.A., Barcelona, 1975, page 162, No. 227.
Catalogue for the Exhibition "Joan Miró. Grafica". Palazzo Pubblico, Siena, 1979, page 90, No. 211.

GALERIE
MAEGHT

MURALES   PEINTURES

MIRO

©MAEGHT EDITEUR IMPRIMEUR

14. MUSÉE NATIONAL D'ART MODERNE EXHIBITION. 1962.

Poster produced for the presentation of 241 works by Joan Miró, at the Musée National d'Art Moderne, Paris (29 June to 4 November, 1962).

Publication:
Indefinite number of copies on standard paper.
Size: 60 × 45 cm.
           160 × 120 cm.

150 copies *avant la lettre* on Rives paper, numbered and signed.
Printing process: colour lithographic press.
Size: 60 × 45 cm.

Publisher: Musée National d'Art Moderne, Paris.
Printer: Arte Adrien Maeght, Paris.

BIBLIOGRAPHY:

Catalogue for the Exhibition "Miró Barcelona 1968-1969". Barcelona City Council, Antiguo Hospital de la Santa Cruz, Barcelona, 1968, page 85, No. 381.
HERRMANNS, Ralph: *Affischer av Miró.* A.H. Grafik, Stockholm, 1974, page 34, No. 9.
Catalogue for the Exhibition "Miró, l'œuvre graphique". Musée d'Art Moderne de la Ville de Paris, 1974, page 140, No. 541.
QUENEAU, Raymond: *Joan Miró Litógrafo II.* Ed. Polígrafa, S.A., Barceona, 1975, page 211, No. 269.
Catalogue for the Exhibition "Joan Miró. Obra Gráfica". Halls of the Dirección General del Patrimonio Artístico, Archivos y Museos, Madrid, 1978, page 81, No. 221.
"Art News", New York, Vol. 78, No. 5, May 1979, page 123.
Catalogue for the Exhibition "Joan Miró. Grafica". Palazzo Pubblico, Siena, 1979, page 90, No. 212.

MIRO.

MUSÉE
NATIONAL
D'ART
MODERNE

29 juin / 4 novembre / de 10 à 17 h sauf mardi / 13 av Pt Wilson

15. "CÉRAMIQUES MONUMENTALES" EXHIBITION. 1963.

Poster for the exhibition of 41 ceramic pieces produced by Miró in collaboration with Llorens Artigas, at the Galerie Maeght, Paris (7 June to July 1963).

Publication:
500 copies on standard paper.
Size: 67 × 50 cm.

200 copies *avant la lettre* on Rives paper, numbered and signed.
Printing process: colour lithographic press.
Size: 67 × 50 cm.

Publisher: Galerie Maeght, Paris.
Printer: Arte Adrien Maeght, Paris.

BIBLIOGRAPHY:

Catalogue for the Exhibition "Miró Barcelona 1968-1969". Barcelona City Council, Antiguo Hospital de la Santa Cruz, Barcelona, 1968, page 85, No. 382.
Catalogue "Derrière le Miroir et Affiches". Maeght Ed., Paris, 1971, page 101, No. 84.
HERRMANNS, Ralph: *Affischer av Miró*. A.H. Grafik, Stockholm, 1974, page 38, No. 11.
Catalogue for the Exhibition "Miró, l'œuvre graphique". Musée d'Art Moderne de la Ville de Paris, 1974, page 140, No. 543.
QUENEAU, Raymond: *Joan Miró Litógrafo II*. Ed. Polígrafa, S.A., Barcelona, 1975, page 212, No. 270.
Catalogue for the Exhibition "Joan Miró. Grafica". Palazzo Pubblico, Siena, 1979, page 90, No. 214.

Galerie Maeght

céramiques monumentales

16. "ALBUM 19". 1963.

Poster produced for the presentation at the Sala Gaspar, Barcelona, of the book *Album 19,* with a text by Raymond Queneau and 26 lithographs by Joan Miró, published by Maeght in Paris (26 October to 15 November 1963).

Publication:
500 copies on standard paper.
Size: 65 × 48 cm.

50 copies *avant la lettre* on Rives paper, numbered and signed.
Printing process: colour lithographic press.
Size: 75.5 × 53 cm.

Publisher: Sala Gaspar, Barcelona.
Printer: Arte Adrien Maeght, Paris.

BIBLIOGRAPHY:

AREAN, Carlos-A.: *Joan Miró*. Publicaciones Españolas. "Cuadernos de Arte", Madrid, 1964, cover.
Catalogue for the Exhibition "Miró Barcelona 1968-1969". Barcelona City Council, Antiguo Hospital de la Santa Cruz, Barcelona, 1968, page 85, No. 383.
HERRMANNS, Ralph: *Affischer av Miró*. A.H. Grafik, Stockholm, 1974, page 35, No. 10.
Catalogue for the Exhibition "Miró, l'œuvre graphique". Musée d'Art Moderne de la Ville de Paris, 1974, page 140, No. 542.
QUENEAU, Raymond: *Joan Miró Litógrafo II*. Ed. Polígrafa, S.A., Barcelona, 1975, page 240, No. 318.
Catalogue for the Exhibition "Joan Miró. Grafica". Palazzo Pubblico, Siena, 1979, page 90, No. 213.

SALA GASPAR · 26·X·15·XI·1963

CONSEJO DE CIENTO, 323 · BARCELONA

17. "THIRTY YEARS OF GRAPHIC ART" EXHIBITION. 1964.

Poster produced for the exhibition of graphic work at the Institute of Contemporary Arts, London (26 August to 10 October 1964).

The composition in green of this poster was taken from the lithograph *Les Guetteurs,* which Miró produced the same year.

Publication:
Indefinite number of copies on standard paper.
Size: 75.5 × 52 cm.

Publisher: Institute of Contemporary Arts, London.
Printer: Arte Adrien Maeght, Paris.

BIBLIOGRAPHY:

HERRMANNS, Ralph: *Affischer av Miró.* A.H. Grafik, Stockholm, 1974, page 39, No. 12.
Catalogue for the Exhibition "Miro, l'œuvre graphique". Musée d'Art Moderne de la Ville de Paris, 1974, page 140, No. 544.
TEIXIDOR, Joan: *Joan Miró Litógrafo III.* Ed. Polígrafa, S.A., Barcelona, 1978, page 58, No. 351.
Catalogue for the Exhibition "Joan Miró. Grafica". Palazzo Pubblico, Siena, 1979, page 90, No. 215.

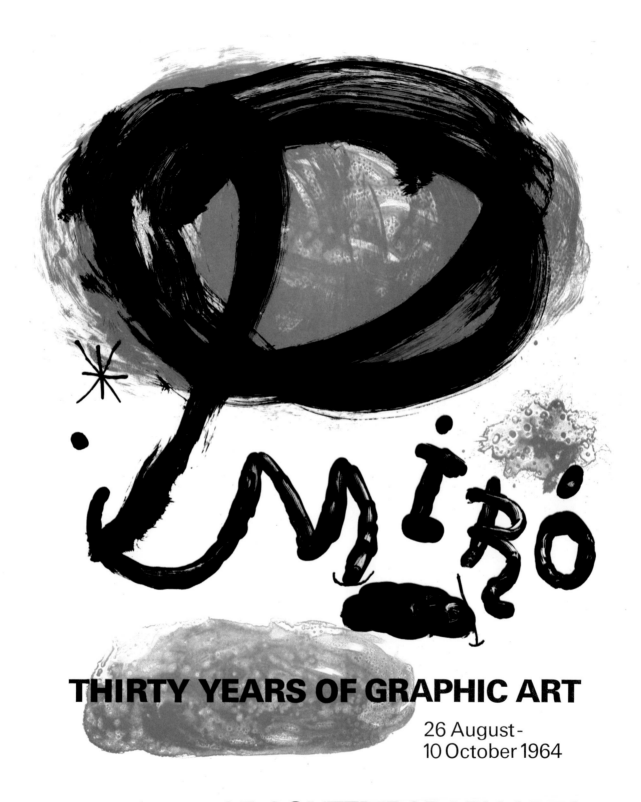

THIRTY YEARS OF GRAPHIC ART

26 August –
10 October 1964

INSTITUTE OF CONTEMPORARY ARTS

17-18 Dover Street W1

open Monday to Friday 10-6   Admission 2/6
Saturdays   10-1   Members free

18. THE TATE GALLERY EXHIBITION, 1964.

Poster produced for the retrospective exhibition of painting, ceramics and sculpture by Joan Miró, at the Tate Gallery, London (28 August to 11 October 1964).

This poster — with its variation in green — was later used for Joan Miró's exhibition at the Kunsthaus, Zürich, (from 31 October to 6 December 1964).

Publication:
Indefinite number of copies on standard paper.
Size: 76 × 50 cm.

Publisher: The Tate Gallery, London.
Printer: Arte Adrien Maeght, Paris.

BIBLIOGRAPHY:

HERRMANNS, Ralph: *Affischer av Miró*. A.H. Grafik, Stockholm, 1974, page 66, No. 31.
Catalogue for the Exhibition "Miró, l'œuvre graphique". Musée d'Art Moderne de la Ville de Paris, 1974, page 140, No. 545.
TEIXIDOR, Joan: *Joan Miró Litógrafo III*. Ed. Polígrafa, S.A., Barcelona, 1978, page 60, No. 353; page 61, No. 354.

The Tate Gallery

An Art Council Exhibition 28th August -
11th October 1964

Admission 3/6d

19. SALA GASPAR-GALERIA METRAS-BELARTE EXHIBITION. 1964.

Poster produced for the exhibition of ceramics, engraved plates and lithographs by Joan Miró, at the Gaspar, Metras and Belarte Galleries, Barcelona (11 to 31 December 1964).

Publication:
1,000 copies on standard paper.
Size: 100 × 70 cm.

50 copies *avant la lettre* on Guarro paper, numbered and signed.
Printing process: colour lithographic press.
Size: 100 × 70 cm.

Publisher: Sala Gaspar, Barcelona.
Printer: Litografías Artísticas Damià Caus, Barcelona.

BIBLIOGRAPHY:

"La Vanguardia Española", Barcelona, 17th December 1964.

"Tele-Exprés", Barcelona, 17th December 1964.

Catalogue for the Exhibition "Miró Barcelona 1968-1969". Barcelona City Council, Antiguo Hospital de la Santa Cruz, Barcelona, page 85, No. 384.

HERRMANNS, Ralph: *Affischer av Miró*. A.H. Grafik, Stockholm, 1974, page 42, No. 13.

Catalogue for the Exhibition "Miró, l'œuvre graphique". Musée d'Art Moderne de la Ville de Paris, 1974, page 140, No. 546.

TEIXIDOR, Joan: *Joan Miró Litógrafo III*. Ed. Polígrafa, S.A., Barcelona, 1978, page 65, No. 355.

Catalogue for the Exhibition "Joan Miró. Obra Gráfica". Halls of the Dirección General del Patrimonio Artístico, Archivos y Museos, Madrid, 1978, page 82, No. 222.

SALA GASPAR
CONSEJO DE CIENTO, 323

GALERIA METRAS
CONSEJO DE CIENTO, 331

BELARTE
CONSEJO DE CIENTO, 353

11 – 31 DICIEMBRE 1964
BARCELONA

20. "CARTONS" EXHIBITION. 1965.

Poster produced for the exhibition of 32 cartoons by Joan Miró at the Galerie Maeght, Paris (4 May to June 1965).

Publication:
Indefinite number of copies on standard paper.
Size: 65.5 × 49 cm.

100 copies *avant la lettre* on Rives paper, numbered and signed.
Printing process: colour lithographic press.
Size: 65.5 × 49 cm.

Publisher: Galerie Maeght, Paris
Printer: Arte Adrien Maeght, Paris.

BIBLIOGRAPHY:

Catalogue for the Exhibition "Miró Barcelona 1968-1969". Barcelona City Council, Antiguo Hospital de la Santa Cruz, Barcelona, 1968, page 85, No. 385.
Catalogue "Derrière le Miroir et Affiches". Maeght Ed., Paris, 1971 page 110, No. 91.
HERRMANNS, Ralph: *Affischer av Miró*. A.H. Grafik, Stockholm, 1974, page 43, No. 14.
Catalogue for the Exhibition "Miró, l'œuvre graphique". Musée d'Art Moderne de la Ville de Paris, 1974, page 140, No. 547.
TEIXIDOR, Joan: *Joan Miró Litógrafo III*. Ed. Polígrafa, S.A., Barcelona, 1978, page 68, No. 358.
Catalogue for the Exhibition "Joan Miró. Grafica". Palazzo Pubblico, Siena, 1979, page 90, No. 216.

GALERIE
MAEGHT

Cartons

MiRo

© Maeght Éditeur Imprimeur

21. "NUITS DE LA FONDATION MAEGHT" EXHIBITION. 1965.

Poster advertising the musical concerts organised by the Maeght Foundation, Saint-Paul-de-Vence (August 1965).

Publication:
Indefinite number of copies on standard paper.
Size: 88.5 × 55.5 cm.

100 copies *avant la lettre* on Arches paper, numbered and signed.

Printing process: colour lithographic press.
Size: 82 × 65 cm.

Publisher: Fondation Maeght, Saint-Paul-de-Vence
Printer: Arte Adrien Maeght, Paris.

BIBLIOGRAPHY:

Catalogue "Affiches-Posters 1979". Maeght Ed., Paris, 1979.

nuits de la fondation maeght

saint-paul (a.m.)

exposition de
musique contemporaine

trois concerts:	4 août 21 h 30	5 août 21 h 30	7 août 21 h 30
	quatuor parrenin **francis pierre**, harpiste œuvres de **berg, debussy, maderna** **miroglio** (1ère audition) **strawinsky**	**yuji takahashi**, pianiste œuvres de **schönberg, cage** **takemitsu** (1ère audition) **boulez, messiaen** **takahashi** (1ère audition) **xenakis**	**geneviève roblot**, soprano **ensemble instrumental** **de musique contemporaine de paris** direction : **konstantin simonovitch** œuvres de **varese, webern, philippot, kotonski** **guézec, stockhausen**

prix des places : 30, 20, 15 et 5 f – abonnement aux 3 concerts : réduction de 10%

| location : fondation maeght
 saint-paul
 32 81 63 | **guglielmi, piano**
 8 rue lépante
 nice
 85 16 24 | **delrieu, disques**
 45 av de la victoire
 nice
 88 61 96 | **syndicat d'initiative**
 13 place masséna
 nice
 85 25 22 | **radio phonola**
 42 bld desmoulins
 monte-carlo
 30 65 26 | **pathé-marconi**
 5 bis pl du général de gaulle
 antibes
 34 02 56 | **delbouis, disques**
 50 bld de la république
 cannes
 38 44 59 |

22. "HOMAGE TO ANTONIO MACHADO". 1966.

Poster produced for the public homage to the poet Antonio Machado, which took place in Baeza, Jaén (20 February 1966).

Publication:
Indefinite number of copies on standard paper.
Size: 72 × 52 cm.

Publisher: Puig Palau, Barcelona.
Printers: Sadagcolor, Barcelona.

BIBLIOGRAPHY:

HERRMANNS, Ralph: *Affischer av Miró*. A.H. Grafik, Stockholm, 1974, page 66, No. 33.
Catalogue for the Exhibition "Miró, l'œuvre graphique". Musée d'Art Moderne de la Ville de Paris, 1974, page 140, No. 551.

1966.

HOMENAJE A ANTONIO MACHADO

BAEZA · 20 febrero 1966

23. "RECENT PAINTINGS 1945-1963" EXHIBITION. 1966.

Poster produced for the exhibition of paintings done by Miró between 1945 and 1963, at the Marlborough Gallery, London (26 April to 28 May 1966).

Publication:
Indefinite number of copies on standard paper.
Size: 74.5 × 50 cm.

Publisher: Marlborough Gallery, London.
Printer: Arte Adrien Maeght, Paris.

BIBLIOGRAPHY:

Catalogue for the Exhibition "Miró Barcelona 1968-1969". Barcelona City Council, Antiguo Hospital de la Santa Cruz, Barcelona, 1968, page 86, No. 390.
HERRMANNS, Ralph: *Affischer av Miró*. A.H. Grafik, Stockholm, 1974, page 46, No. 15.
Catalogue for the Exhibition "Miró, l'œuvre graphique". Musée d'Art Moderne de la Ville de Paris, 1974, page 140, No. 548.
TEIXIDOR, Joan: *Joan Miró Litógrafo III*. Ed. Polígrafa, S.A., Barcelona, 1978, page 103, No. 433.
Catalogue for the Exhibition "Joan Miró. Grafica". Palazzo Pubblico, Siena, 1979, page 90, No. 217.

MARLBOROUGH

39 Old Bond Street, London W1

IMPRIMERIE ARTE PARIS

Recent paintings 1945-1963

26th April - 28th May 1966

24. "XXII SALON DE MAI" EXHIBITION. 1966.

Poster produced for the 22nd *Salon de Mai,* held at the Musée d'Art Moderne de la Ville de Paris (2 to 22 May 1966).

Publication:
Indefinite number of copies on standard paper.
Size: 67.5 × 50 cm.

100 copies *avant la lettre* on Arches paper, numbered and signed.
The original lithograph of the poster *avant la lettre* has been modified and embellished by Joan Miró.

Printing process: colour lithographic press.
Size: 67 × 52 cm.

Publisher: Salon de Mai, Paris.
Printer: Mourlot, Paris.

BIBLIOGRAPHY:

Catalogue for the Exhibition "Miró Barcelona 1968-1969". Barcelona City Council, Antiguo Hospital de la Santa Cruz, Barcelona, 1968, page 85, No. 387.
TAILLANDIER, Yvon: *Mirografías.* Ed. Gustavo Gili, S.A., Barcelona, 1972, page 189.
HERRMANNS, Ralph: *Affischer av Miró.* A.H. Grafik, Stockholm, 1974, page 47, No. 16.
Catalogue for the Exhibition "Miró, l'œuvre graphique". Musée d'Art Moderne de la Ville de Paris, 1974, page 140, No. 550.
TEIXIDOR, Joan: *Joan Miró Litógrafo III.* Ed. Polígrafa, S.A., Barcelona, 1978, page 101, No. 431; page 102, No. 432.
Catalogue for the Exhibition "Joan Miró. Grafica". Palazzo Pubblico, Siena, 1979, page 90. No. 218.

MUSÉE D'ART MODERNE DE LA VILLE DE PARIS

SALON DE MAI
XXIIᵉ SALON - DU 2 AU 22 MAI 1966

25. "MERCE CUNNINGHAM AND DANCE COMPANY". 1966.

Poster produced by Miró for the presentation of the Merce Cunningham dance group at the Prado Theatre in Sitges, Barcelona (29 July 1966).

Publication:
1,000 copies on standard paper.
Size: 72 × 50 cm.

200 copies *avant la lettre* on standard paper, numbered and signed.
Printing process: colour photoreproduction.
Size: 72 × 50 cm.

Publisher: Club 49, Barcelona.
Printer: Foto Repro, Barcelona.

BIBLIOGRAPHY:

Catalogue for the Exhibition "Miró Barcelona 1968-1969". Barcelona City Council. Antiguo Hospital de la Santa Cruz, Barcelona, 1968, page 86, No. 394.
HERRMANNS, Ralph: *Affischer av Miró*. A.H. Grafik, Stockholm, 1974, page 66, No. 34.
Catalogue for the Exhibition "Miró, l'œuvre graphique". Musée d'Art Moderne de la Ville de Paris, 1974, page 140, No. 552.
RAILLARD, Georges: *Joan Miró. Ceci est la couleur de mes rêves*. Ed. du Seuil, Paris, 1977, page 99.
Catalogue for the Exhibition "Joan Miró. Gráfica". Halls of the Dirección General del Patrimonio Artístico, Archivos y Museos, Madrid, 1978, page 82, No. 223.

MERCE CUNNINGHAM AND DANCE COMPANY

JOHN CAGE, DAVID TUDOR

CLUB 49   29-VII-1966   SITGES

26. "JOAN MIRÓ GRAPHICS" EXHIBITION. 1966.

Poster produced for the exhibition of graphic work and books illustrated by Joan Miró, at the Philadelphia Museum of Art, Philadelphia (15 September to 23 October 1966).

Publication:
200 copies on standard paper.
Size: 76 × 56 cm.
There are reprints of this poster.

150 copies *avant la lettre* on Arches paper, numbered and signed.
Printing process: colour lithographic press.
Size: 76 × 56 cm.

Publisher: Philadelphia Museum of Art, Philadelphia.
Printer: Arte Adrien Maeght, Paris.

BIBLIOGRAPHY:

Catalogue for the Exhibition "Joan Miró: Prints and Books". Philadelphia Museum of Art, Philadelphia, 1966.
Catalogue for the Exhibition "Miró Barcelona 1968-1969". Barcelona City Council, Antiguo Hospital de la Santa Cruz, Barcelona, 1968, page 85, No. 389.
HERRMANNS, Ralph: *Affischer av. Miró.* A.H. Grafik, Stockholm, 1974, page 66, No. 36.
Catalogue for the Exhibition "Miró, l'œuvre graphique". Musée d'Art Moderne de la Ville de Paris, 1974, page 140, No. 553.
TEIXIDOR, Joan: *Joan Miró Litógrafo III.* Ed. Polígrafa, S.A., Barcelona, 1978, page 104, No. 434.

27. "L'OISEAU SOLAIRE, L'OISEAU LUNAIRE, ÉTINCELLES"
EXHIBITION. 1967.

Poster produced for the Miró exhibition "L'oiseau solaire, l'oiseau lunaire,
étincelles", held at the Galerie Maeght, Paris (April 1967).

Publication:
Indefinite number of copies on standard paper.
Size: 64.5 × 48 cm.

150 copies *avant la lettre* on Lana paper, numbered and signed.
Printing process: colour lithographic press.
Size: 64.5 × 48 cm.

Publisher: Galerie Maeght, Paris.
Printer: Arte Adrien Maeght, Paris.

BIBLIOGRAPHY:

Catalogue for the Exhibition "Miró Barcelona 1968-1969". Barcelona City Council, Antiguo
Hospital de la Santa Cruz, Barcelona, 1968, page 86, No. 391.
Catalogue "Derrière le Miroir et Affiches". Maeght Ed., Paris, 1971, page 121, No. 101.
HERRMANNS, Ralph: *Affischer av Miró*. A.H. Grafik, Stockholm, 1974, page 67, No. 37.
Catalogue for the Exhibition "Miró, l'œuvre graphique". Musée d'Art Moderne de la Ville de Paris,
1974, page 140, No. 554.
TEIXIDOR, Joan: *Joan Miró Litógrafo III*. Ed. Polígrafa, S.A., Barcelona, 1978, page 107. No. 438.

GALERIE MAEGHT

13 rue de Téhéran

l'oiseau solaire

l'oiseau lunaire

étincelles

28. "L'OISEAU SOLAIRE, L'OISEAU LUNAIRE, ÉTINCELLES" EXHIBITION. 1967.

Large-scale poster produced for Miró's exhibition "L'oiseau solaire, l'oiseau lunaire, étincelles", held at the Galerie Maeght, Paris (April 1967).

Publication:
Indefinite number of copies on standard paper.
Size: 160 × 120 cm.

Publisher: Galerie Maeght, Paris.
Printer: Arte Adrien Maeght, Paris.

BIBLIOGRAPHY:

PERUCHO, Juan: *Joan Miró y Cataluña.* Ed. Polígrafa, S.A., Barcelona, 1968, page 217.
Catalogue for the Exhibition "Miró, l'œuvre graphique". Musée d'Art Moderne de la Ville de Paris, 1974, page 140, No. 555.
TEIXIDOR, Joan: *Joan Miró Litógrafo III,* Ed. Polígrafa, S.A., Barcelona, 1978, page 106, No. 437.

GALERIE
MAEGHT

13 rue de Téhéran
Paris 8

l'oiseau solaire
l'oiseau lunaire
étincelles

29. "ATELIER MOURLOT". 1967.

Poster produced for the opening of the printer Fernand Mourlot's atelier in New York.

Publication:
Indefinite number of copies on standard paper.
Size: 71 × 53.5 cm.

60 copies *avant la lettre,* on Rives paper, modified by Joan Miró, numbered and signed.
Printing process: colour lithographic press.
Size: 68 × 51 cm.

Publisher: Mourlot, Paris.
Printer: Mourlot, New York.

BIBLIOGRAPHY:

HERRMANNS, Ralph: *Affischer av Miró.* A.H. Grafik, Stockholm, 1974, page 51, No. 18.
Catalogue for the Exhibition "Miró, l'œuvre graphique". Musée d'Art Moderne de la Ville de Paris, 1974, page 140, No. 549.
TEIXIDOR, Joan: *Joan Miró Litógrafo III.* Ed. Polígrafa, S.A., Barcelona, 1978, page 111, No. 443; page 112, No. 444.

ATELIER MOURLOT

115 BANK STREET - NEW YORK - NY 10014

ATELIER MOURLOT LTD

30. "1.er DE MAIG 1968". 1968.

Poster produced by Miró for the commemoration in Barcelona of 1st May.

Publication:
15,000 copies on standard paper.
Size: 64.5 × 49.5 cm.

Publisher: Comisiones Obreras, Barcelona.
Printer: Gráficas Casamajó, Barcelona.

BIBLIOGRAPHY:

"Avui", Barcelona, 20 April 1978.
HERRMANNS, Ralph: *Affischer av Miró.* A.H. Grafik, Stockholm, 1974, page 54, No. 19.
JOHANSSON, Kjell A.: *Miró en Escania.* "Dagens Nyheter", Stockholm, 30 June 1976.
"L'avenç", Barcelona, No. 16, May 1979, page 71.

31. "SALVAT CATALÀ". 1968.

Poster produced for the presentation of the four-volume encyclopedia *Diccionari Enciclopèdic-Salvat Català*.

Publication:
200,000 copies on standard paper.
Size: 47 × 61.5 cm.

400 copies on standard paper.
Size: 300 × 400 cm.

200 copies *avant la lettre* on special paper.
Printing process: colour offset.
Size: 45 × 60 cm.

Publisher: Salvat Editores, S.A., Barcelona.
Printer: Imprenta Hispano-Americana, S.A., Barcelona.

BIBLIOGRAPHY:

Catalogue for the Exhibition "Miró Barcelona 1968-1969". Barcelona City Council, Antiguo Hospital de la Santa Cruz, Barcelona, 1968, page 86, No. 395.
MELIÀ, Josep: *Joan Miró*. Ed. Dopesa, Barcelona, 1971, pages 62-63.
"El Noticiero Universal", Barcelona, 12 November 1974.
CLEMENTE, Josep Carles: *Miró invade las calles de Barcelona*. "Gaceta del Arte", Madrid, Year III, No. 35, 15 January 1975, page 4.

Diccionari Enciclopèdic en 4 volums, en fascicles setmanals

TOTS L'HEM DE CONEIXER

32. "MIRÓ, FONDATION MAEGHT" EXHIBITION. 1968.

Poster produced for Miró's retrospective exhibition at the Maeght Foundation, Saint-Paul-de-Vence, to celebrate the painter's 75th birthday (23 July to 30 September 1968).

This poster was later used for the exhibition "Miró Barcelona 1968-1969", organised by Barcelona City Council, at the Antiguo Hospital de la Santa Cruz (November 1968-January 1969).

Publication:
Indefinite number of copies on standard paper.
Size: 74 × 51.5 cm.

125 copies *avant la lettre* on Arches paper, numbered and signed.
Printing process: colour lithographic press.
Size: 85 × 61 cm.

Publisher: Fondation Adrien Maeght, Saint-Paul-de-Vence.
Printer: Arte Adrien Maeght, Paris.

From the poster for the exhibition in Barcelona 1,000 numbered copies were run off, printed by Sadagcolor, Barcelona.

BIBLIOGRAPHY:

Catalogue for the Exhibition "Miró Barcelona 1968-1969". Barcelona City Council, Antiguo Hospital de la Santa Cruz, Barcelona, 1968, page 86, No. 392.
"Diario de Barcelona". Barcelona, 17 November 1968.
"El Noticiero Universal", Barcelona, 27 November 1968.
HERRMANNS, Ralph: *Affischer av Miró*. A.H. Grafik, Stockholm, 1974, page 67, No. 39.
Catalogue for the Exhibition "Miró, l'œuvre graphique". Musée d'Art Moderne de la Ville de Paris, 1974, page 140, No. 556.
TEIXIDOR, Joan: *Joan Miró Litógrafo III*. Ed. Polígrafa, S.A., Barcelona, 1978, page, 157, No. 502.
Catalogue for the Exhibition "Joan Miró. Obra Gráfica". Halls of the Dirección General del Patrimonio Artístico. Archivos y Museos, Madrid, 1978, page 82, No. 224.
Catalogue "Affiches-Posters 1979". Maeght Ed., Paris, 1979.

DU 23 JUILLET AU 30 SEPTEMBRE 1968 SAINT-PAUL 06

FONDATION MAEGHT

33. "2 LLIBRES: JOAN MIRÓ I CATALUNYA-LES ESSÈNCIES DE LA TERRA" EXHIBITION. 1968.

Poster produced for the presentation at the Sala Gaspar, Barcelona, of the books *Joan Miró i Catalunya* and *Les essències de la terra,* published by Ed. Polígrafa, S.A., Barcelona (3 October 1968).

Publication:
500 copies on standard paper.
1,000 copies on Guarro paper, numbered and stamped.
Size: 77 × 55 cm.

Publisher: Ed. Polígrafa, S.A., Barcelona.
Printer: La Polígrafa, S.A., Barcelona.

BIBLIOGRAPHY:

Catalogue for the Exhibition "Miró Barcelona 1968-1969". Barcelona City Council, Antiguo Hospital de la Santa Cruz, Barcelona, 1968, page 86, No. 393.
HERRMANNS, Ralph: *Affischer av Miró.* A.H. Grafik, Stockholm, 1974, page 67, No. 38.

SALA GASPAR

2 LLIBRES

JOAN MIRO i CATALUNYA

LES ESSÈNCIES DE LA TERRA...

OCTUBRE 1968 - BARCELONA

34. "CONCURS CENTENARI POMPEU FABRA" EXHIBITION. 1968.

Poster planned for the competition organized in Barcelona in honour of the centenary of the birth of the Catalan philologist Pompeu Fabra.

Drawing in India ink on paper, 22 × 22 cm.

Comissió Pompeu Fabra Collection, Barcelona.

BIBLIOGRAPHY:

Catalogue for the Exhibition "Miró Barcelona 1968-1969". Barcelona .City Council, Antiguo Hospital de la Santa Cruz, Barcelona, 1968, page 72, No. 172, plate 39.

35. "MIRÓ BARCELONA 1968-1969" EXHIBITION. 1968.

Poster planned for the exhibition "Miró Barcelona 1968-1969", organised by Barcelona City Council.

Gouache on paper, 34 × 27 cm.

Fundació Joan Miró Collection, Barcelona.

BIBLIOGRAPHY:

Catalogue for the Exhibition "Miró Barcelona 1968-1969". Barcelona City Council, Antiguo Hospital de la Santa Cruz, Barcelona, 1968, page 72, No. 171, plate 38.
"La Prensa", Barcelona, 17 January 1969.

36. PASADENA ART MUSEUM EXHIBITION. 1969.

Poster produced for the retrospective exhibition of Joan Miró's graphic work, held at the Pasadena Art Museum, California, U.S.A.

Publication:
Indefinite number of copies on standard paper.
Size: 80.5 × 56.5 cm.

100 copies *avant la lettre* on Arches paper, numbered and signed.
Printing process: colour lithographic press.

Publisher: Pasadena Art Museum, Pasadena.
Printer: Mourlot, Paris.

BIBLIOGRAPHY:

Catalogue for the Exhibition "Miro: selected graphics". Berggruen Gallery, San Francisco, 1970.
HERRMANNS, Ralph: *Affischer av Miró*. A.H. Grafik, Stockholm, 1974, page 55, No. 20.
Catalogue for the Exhibition "Miró, l'œuvre graphique". Musée d'Art Moderne de la Ville de Paris, 1974, page 142, No. 559.
TEIXIDOR, Joan: *Joan Miró Litógrafo III,* Ed. Polígrafa, S.A., Barcelona, 1978, page 206, No. 554.

PASADENA ART MUSEUM

37. PRESENTATION IN MILAN OF THE BOOKS "JOAN MIRÓ Y CATALUÑA" AND "LES ESSÈNCIES DE LA TERRA". 1969.

Poster produced for the presentation at the Galleria Il Milione in Milan of the books *Joan Miró y Cataluña* and *Les essències de la Terra,* published by Ed. Polígrafa, S.A., Barcelona (29 May to 28 June 1969).

Publication:
1,000 copies on standard paper.
Size: 75.5 × 58 cm.

140 copies *avant la lettre* on Guarro paper, numbered and monogrammed.
200 copies *avant la lettre* on special paper, numbered and monogrammed.
Printing process: colour lithographic press.
Size: 76 × 58 cm.

Publisher: Ed. Polígrafa, S.A., Barcelona.
Printer: La Polígrafa, S.A., Barcelona

BIBLIOGRAPHY:

Catalogue for the Exhibition "Miró: selected graphics". Berggruen Gallery, San Francisco, 1970.
HERRMANNS, Ralph: *Affischer av Miró.* A.H. Grafik, Stockholm, 1974, page 67, No. 41.
Catalogue for the Exhibition "Miró, l'œuvre graphique". Musée d'Art Moderne de la Ville de Paris, 1974, page 142, No. 560.

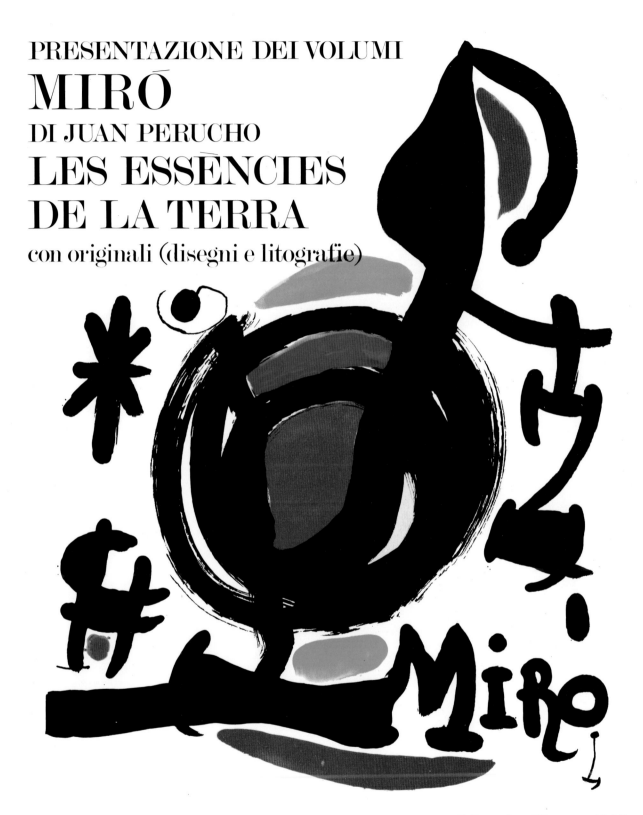

PRESENTAZIONE DEI VOLUMI
MIRÓ
DI JUAN PERUCHO
LES ESSÈNCIES
DE LA TERRA
con originali (disegni e litografie)

AL MILIONE

Maggio-Giugno 1969
21 via Bigli • Milano

38. "ŒUVRE GRAVÉ ET LITHOGRAPHIÉ" EXHIBITION. 1969.

Poster produced for the exhibition of Miró's graphic work, at the Galerie Gérald Cramer, Geneva (9 June to 27 September 1969).

Publication:
Indefinite number of copies on standard paper.
Size: 65 × 50 cm.

75 copies *avant la lettre* on Rives paper, numbered and signed.
Printing process: colour lithographic press.
Size: 78 × 55.5 cm.

Publisher: Galerie Gérald Cramer, Geneva.
Printer: Arte Adrien Maeght, Paris.

BIBLIOGRAPHY:

Catalogue for the Exhibition "Œuvre gravé et lithographié". Galerie Gérald Cramer, Geneva, 1969, page 25, No. 51.
TAILLANDIER, Yvon: *Mirografías,* Ed. Gustavo Gili, S.A., Barcelona, 1972, page 191.
HERRMANNS, Ralph: *Affischer av Miró.* A.H. Grafik, Stockholm, 1974, page 67, No. 40.
Catalogue for the Exhibition "Miró, l'œuvre graphique". Musée d'Art Moderne de la Ville de Paris, 1974, page 142, No. 558.

39. "DONAUESCHINGER MUSIKTAGE", 1969.

Poster produced for the music congress in Donaueschingen, West Germany, held on 18 and 19 October 1969.

Publication:
Indefinite number of copies on standard paper.
Size: 88 × 59 cm.

Publisher: Städtisches Kulturamt, Donaueschingen.
Printer: Arte Adrien Maeght, Paris.

75 copies *avant la lettre* on Rives paper, numbered and signed; edition called *Variante II.*

75 copies *avant la lettre,* with the modification of some of the colours by Miró, on Rives paper, numbered and signed; edition called *Variante I.*
Printing process: colour lithographic press.
Size: 90 × 61 cm.

Publisher: Galerie Maeght, Paris.
Printer: Arte Adrien Maeght, Paris.

BIBLIOGRAPHY:

Catalogue for the Exhibition "Miró". Galleria d'Arte La Bussola, Turin, 1970, page 53, No. 59.
HERRMANNS, Ralph: *Affischer av Miró.* A.H. Grafik, Stockholm, 1974, page 58, No. 21.
TEIXIDOR, Joan: *Joan Miró Litógrafo III.* Ed. Polígrafa, S.A., Barcelona, 1978, page 170, No. 518; page 171, No, 519.

Donaueschinger Musiktage

18./19. Oktober 1969

Auskunft-Kartenvorbestellung: Städtisches Kulturamt·771 Donaueschingen
Telefon (0771) 3014

Entwurf: Juan Miró   Druck: Galerie Maeght·Paris

40. PRESENTATION OF THREE BOOKS ON MIRÓ IN JAPAN. 1970.

Poster produced for the presentation in Osaka, Japan, of the book on Miró's work *Joan Miró y Catalunya,* along with *Les essències de la terra* and *Mà de proverbis,* illustrated by Miró and all published by Ed. Polígrafa, S. A., Barcelona.

This poster was later used for the exhibition of lithographs at the Galerie Hachette, London (22 January to 20 February 1971).

Publication:
2,000 copies on standard paper.
Size: 76 × 56.6 cm.
There is also a publication of the same poster with Catalan text.

500 copies *avant la lettre* on Guarro paper, numbered and monogrammed.
Printing process: colour lithographic press.
Size: 76 × 56.5 cm.

Publisher: Ed. Polígrafa, S.A., Barcelona.
Printer: La Polígrafa, S.A., Barcelona.

BIBLIOGRAPHY:

HERRMANNS, Ralph: *La nit i el somni, pintar com Miró.* Ed. Bonnier, Stockholm, 1972.
HERRMANNS, Ralph: *Affischer av Miró.* A.H. Grafik, Stockholm, 1974, page 68, No. 43.
Catalogue for the Exhibition "Miró, l'oeuvre graphique". Musée d'Art Moderne de la Ville de Paris, 1974, page 142, No. 564.
Catalogue for the Exhibition "Joan Miró. Obra Gráfica". Halls of the Dirección General del Patrimonio Artístico, Archivos y Museos, Madrid, 1978, page 82, No. 225.
Catalogue for the Exhibition "Joan Miró. Grafica". Palazzo Pubblico, Siena, 1979, pages 90-91, No. 219.

ジョアン・ミロの3冊の本

ジョアン・ミロとカタロニア
フォトスコープ・ミロ
手づくり諺

41. "SCULPTURES" EXHIBITION. 1970.

Poster produced for the exhibition of Miró's sculptures held at the Galerie Maeght, Paris (23 July to 30 September 1970).

Publication:
Indefinite number of copies on standard paper.
Size: 77 × 54 cm.

150 copies *avant la lettre* on Lana paper, numbered and signed.
Printing process: colour lithographic press.
Size: 77 × 54 cm.

Publisher: Galerie Maeght, Paris.
Printer: Arte Adrien Maeght, Paris.

BIBLIOGRAPHY:

Catalogue "Derrière le Miroir et Affiches". Maeght Ed., Paris, page 142, No. 121.
HERRMANNS, Ralph: *Affischer av Miró*. A.H. Grafik, Stockholm, 1974, page 67, No. 42.
Catalogue for the Exhibition "Miró, l'oeuvre graphique". Musée d'Art Moderne de la Ville de Paris, 1974, page 142, No. 561.
"Art News", New York, Vol. 76, No. 8, October 1977, page 122.

42. "SCULPTURES" EXHIBITION. 1970.

Poster produced for the exhibition of Miró's sculptures held at the Galerie Maeght, Paris (23 July to 30 September 1970).

Publication:
Indefinite number of copies on standard paper.
Size: 160 × 120 cm.

Publisher: Galerie Maeght, Paris.
Printer: Arte Adrien Maeght, Paris.

BIBLIOGRAPHY:

Catalogue for the Exhibition "Miró, l'oeuvre graphique". Musée d'Art Moderne de la Ville de Paris, 1974, page 142, No. 562.

Galerie
Maeght

MIRÓ.

sculptures

43. "MIRÓ, SALA GASPAR-BARCELONA" EXHIBITION. 1970.

Poster for the presentation at the Sala Gaspar, Barcelona of the cartoon and the tapestry produced by Miró for the Hospital de la Cruz Roja, Tarragona (September 1970).

Publication:
500 copies on standard paper.
Size: 75 × 55.5 cm.

200 copies *avant la lettre* on Guarro paper, numbered and monogrammed.
Printing process: colour lithographic press.
Size: 75 × 55.5 cm.

Publisher: Sala Gaspar, Barcelona.
Printer: Publicaciones Reunidas, S.A., Barcelona.

BIBLIOGRAPHY:

HERRMANNS, Ralph: *Affischer av Miró*. A.H. Grafik, Stockholm, 1974, page 68, No. 44.
Catalogue for the Exhibition "Miró, l'oeuvre graphique". Musée d'Art Moderne de la Ville de Paris, 1974, page 142, No. 565.

BARCELONA - SETEMBRE - 1970

SALA GASPAR

DEPOSITO LEGAL B·31.376·70

44. "MIRÓ SALA PELAIRES" EXHIBITION. 1970.

Poster published for an exhibition of Miró's original work at the Sala Pelaires, Palma de Mallorca (October 1970).

Publication:
1,000 copies on standard paper.
Size: 75 × 55.5 cm.

75 copies *avant la lettre* on Guarro paper, numbered and signed.
Printing process: colour lithographic press.
Size: 75 × 55.5 cm.

Publisher: Sala Pelaires, Palma de Mallorca.
Printer: Publicaciones Reunidas, S.A., Barcelona.

BIBLIOGRAPHY:

HERRMANNS, Ralph: *Affischer av Miró*. A.H. Grafik, Stockholm, 1974, page 68, No. 45.
Catalogue for the Exhibition "Miró, l'oeuvre graphique". Musée d'Art Moderne de la Ville de Paris, 1974, page 142, No. 563.

PALMA DE MALLORCA - OCTUBRE - 1970

SALA PELAIRES

DEPOSITO LEGAL: B - 31.375 - 70   PUBLICACIONES REUNIDAS S.A. - BARCELONA

45. "LLORENS ARTIGAS-JOANET ARTIGAS" EXHIBITION. 1971.

Poster produced by Miró for the exhibition of the ceramists Josep Llorens Artigas and his son Joan, at the Sala Pelaires, Palma de Mallorca (April 1971).

Publication:
1,000 copies on standard paper.
Size: 75.5 × 56 cm.

100 copies *avant la lettre* on Arches paper, numbered and signed.
Printing process: colour lithographic press.
Size: 90 × 63 cm.

Publisher: Sala Pelaires, Palma de Mallorca.
Printer: Arte Adrien Maeght, Paris.

BIBLIOGRAPHY:

HERRMANNS, Ralph: *Affischer av Miró*. A.H. Grafik, Stockholm, 1974, page 68, No. 46.
Catalogue for the Exhibition "Miró, l'oeuvre graphique". Musée d'Art Moderne de la Ville de Paris, 1974, page 142, No. 567.

SALA PELAIRES

46. "1.ª MUESTRA INTERNACIONAL DE ARTE. HOMENAJE A JOAN MIRÓ" EXHIBITION. 1971.

Poster produced for the exhibition in homage to Joan Miró, organised in Granollers, Barcelona (15 May to 15 September 1971).
This composition was used as a cover for the catalogue published for this exhibition.

Publication:
2,000 copies on Guarro paper.
Size: 76 × 55.5 cm.

Publisher: Granollers Town Council (Barcelona).
Printer: La Polígrafa, S.A., Barcelona.

1ª Muestra Internacional de Arte HOMENAJE a JOAN MIRÓ Granollers

15 de Mayo - 15 de Septiembre 1971

47. "AGORA 1" EXHIBITION. 1971.

Poster produced for the presentation of Galerie Maeght artists in Paris, at the Musée d'Art Moderne, Strasbourg (13 July to 30 September 1971).

Publication:
Indefinite number of copies on standard paper.
Size: 120 × 78 cm.
     60 × 40 cm.

125 copies *avant la lettre* on Arches paper, numbered and signed.
Printing process: colour lithographic press.
Size: 89 × 78 cm.

Publisher: Musée d'Art Moderne, Strasbourg.
Printer: Arte Adrien Maeght, Paris.

BIBLIOGRAPHY:

Catalogue for the Exhibition "Miró Opere Grafiche Originali". Galleria Ciranna, Milan, 1972, No. 37.
HERRMANNS, Ralph: *Affischer av Miró*. A.H. Grafik, Stockholm, 1974, page 68, No. 47.
Catalogue for the Exhibition "Miró, l'œuvre graphique". Musée d'Art Moderne de la Ville de Paris, 1974, page 142, No. 566.

AGORA 1

STRASBOURG

MUSÉE D'ART MODERNE, ANCIENNE DOUANE
DU 13 JUILLET AU 30 SEPTEMBRE 1971

ARTISTES DE LA GALERIE MAEGHT : BONNARD . KANDINSKY .
BRAQUE . CHAGALL . GIACOMETTI . LEGER . MIRÓ . CALDER .
LLORENS ARTIGAS . BRAM VAN VELDE . GEER VAN VELDE .
BAZAINE . UBAC . TAL-COAT . STEINBERG . KEMENY . CHILLIDA .
PALAZUELO . TÀPIES . RIOPELLE . BURY . REBEYROLLE . KELLY .
ADAMI . LE YAOUANC . GARDY ARTIGAS . GARACHE .

48. "HOMENATGE A JOAN PRATS" EXHIBITION. 1971.

Poster for the presentation of the series of 15 lithographs *Homenatge a Joan Prats,* produced by Miró and published by Ed. Polígrafa, S.A., at the Sala Gaspar, Barcelona (28 September to October 1971).

This poster was used between 1972 and 1973 for the presentation of this series of lithographs in the following galleries and museums: Galería Vandrés, Madrid; Galería Juana de Aizpuru, Seville; Galería Carl van der Voort, Ibiza; Sala Pelaires, Palma de Mallorca; Museu de l'Empordà, Figueras (Gerona); Galerie Bonnier, Geneva; Galerie Ziegler, Zürich; Galerie Dreiseitel, Cologne; Svensk-Franska Konstgalleriet, Stockholm; and Arras Gallery, New York.

Publication:
1,000 copies on standard paper.
Size: 75.5 × 56 cm.

150 copies *avant la lettre* on Guarro paper, numbered and signed.
Printing process: colour lithographic press.
Size: 75.5 × 56 cm.

Publisher: Ed. Polígrafa, S.A., Barcelona.
Printer: La Polígrafa, S.A., Barcelona.

BIBLIOGRAPHY:

HERRMANNS, Ralph: *Affischer av Miró*. A.H. Grafik, Stockholm, 1974, page 68, No. 48.
Catalogue for the Exhibition "Miró, l'œuvre graphique". Musée d'Art Moderne de la Ville de Paris, 1974, page 142, No. 571.
Catalogue for the Exhibition "Joan Miró. Obra Gráfica". Halls of the Dirección General del Patrimonio Artístico, Archivos y Museos, Madrid, 1978, page 82, No. 226.
Catalogue for the Exhibition "Joan Miró. Obra Gràfica". Exhibition Room of the Caixa d'Estalvis Laietana, Mataró (Barcelona), 1978, No. 30.
Catalogue for the Exhibition "Joan Miró. Grafica". Palazzo Pubblico, Siena, 1979, page 91, No. 220.

SALA GASPAR

BARCELONA - SETEMBRE - OCTUBRE · 1971

49. "MIRÓ SCULPTURES" EXHIBITION. 1971.

Poster produced for the exhibition of 90 Miró sculptures at the Walker Art Center, Minneapolis (3 October to 28 November 1971).

This poster was later used for the exhibition of these same works at the Cleveland Museum of Art (2 February to 12 March 1972) and at the Chicago Art Institute (15 April to 28 May 1972).

Publication:
Indefinite number of copies on standard paper.
Size: 116 × 76 cm.

150 copies *avant la lettre* on Arches paper, numbered and signed.
Printing process: colour lithographic press.
Size: 85.5 × 73 cm.

Publisher: Walker Art Center, Minneapolis.
Printer: Arte Adrien Maeght, Paris.

BIBLIOGRAPHY:

HERRMANNS, Ralph: *Affischer av Miró*. A.H. Grafik, Stockholm, 1974, page 69, No. 52.
Catalogue for the Exhibition "Miró, l'œuvre graphique". Musée d'Art Moderne de la Ville de Paris, 1974, page 143, No. 578.

MIRÓ SCULPTURES

WALKER ART CENTER 3 OCT-28 NOV 1971

50. "II CONGRESO JURÍDICO CATALÁN". 1971.

Poster produced by Miró for the *II Congreso Jurídico Catalán,* organised by the Colegio de Abogados, Barcelona (October to November 1971).

Publication:
1,000 copies on standard paper.
Size: 77 × 57 cm.

50 copies *avant la lettre* on Guarro paper, signed.
Printing process: colour offset.
Size: 76.5 × 58 cm.

Publisher: Colegio de Abogados de Barcelona.
Printer: La Polígrafa, S.A., Barcelona.

BIBLIOGRAPHY:

HERRMANNS, Ralph: *Affischer av Miró.* A.H Grafik, Stockholm, 1974, page 69, No. 50.
Catalogue for the Exhibition "Miró, l'œuvre graphique". Musée d'Art Moderne de la Ville de Paris, 1974, page 142, No. 572.
JOHANSSON, Kjell A.: *Miró en Escania.* "Dagens Nyheter", Stockholm, 30 June 1976.
"Avui", Barcelona, 20 April 1978, page 14.

II CONGRESO JURIDICO
CATALAN OCTUBRE - NOVBRE. 1971

51. "PEINTURES SUR PAPIER-DESSINS" EXHIBITION. 1971.

Poster produced for two successive Miró exhibitions at the Galerie Maeght, Paris: *Peintures sur papier* (15 October to 12 November 1971) and *Dessins* (17 November to 6 December 1971).

Publication:
Indefinite number of copies on standard paper.
Size: 80 × 56 cm.

150 copies *avant la lettre* on Arches paper, numbered and signed.
Printing process: colour lithographic press.
Size: 85 × 59 cm.

Publisher: Galerie Maeght, Paris.
Printer: Arte Adrien Maeght, Paris.

BIBLIOGRAPHY:

Catalogue for the Exhibition "Miró Opere Grafiche Originali". Galleria Ciranna, Milan, 1972, No. 38.
Supplementary catalogue "Maeght Éditeur 1973". Paris, 1973, page 147, No. 128.
HERRMANNS, Ralph: *Affischer av Miró*. A.H. Grafik, Stockholm, 1974, page 69, No. 51.
Catalogue for the Exhibition "Miró, l'œuvre graphique". Musée d'Art Moderne de la Ville de Paris, 1974, page 142, No. 569.

GALERIE MAEGHT

13 RUE DE TÉHÉRAN PARIS 8

15 OCTOBRE/12 NOVEMBRE : PEINTURES SUR PAPIER

17 NOVEMBRE/6 DÉCEMBRE : DESSINS

52. "PEINTURES SUR PAPIER-DESSINS" EXHIBITION. 1971.

Large-scale poster produced for two successive Miró exhibitions at the Galerie Maeght, Paris: *Peintures sur papier* (15 October to 12 November 1971) and *Dessins* (17 November to 6 December 1971).

Publication:
Indefinite number of copies on standard paper.
Size: 160 × 120 cm.

50 copies *avant la lettre* on Arches paper, numbered and signed.
Printing process: colour lithographic press.
Size: 160 × 120 cm.

Publisher: Galerie Maeght, Paris.
Printer: Arte Adrien Maeght, Paris.

BIBLIOGRAPHY:

Catalogue for the Exhibition "Miró, l'œuvre graphique". Musée d'Art Moderne de la Ville de Paris, 1974, page 142, No. 570.

GALERIE MAEGHT

13 RUE DE TÉHÉRAN PARIS 8

15 OCTOBRE / 12 NOVEMBRE : PEINTURES SUR PAPIER

17 NOVEMBRE / 6 DÉCEMBRE : DESSINS

MIRO.

53. "LE LÉZARD AUX PLUMES D'OR". 1971

Poster produced for the presentation at the Galerie Berggruen, Paris (23 November to 31 December 1971), and at the Galerie Pierre, Stockholm (4 December-31 December 1971), of the poem *Le lézard aux plumes d'or* by Joan Miró, illustrated by the painter himself and published by Louis Broder in Paris.

Publication:
Indefinite number of copies on standard paper.
Size: 70 × 49.5 cm.

150 copies *avant la lettre* and modified by Miró on Arches paper, numbered and signed.
Printing process: colour lithographic press.
Size: 66 × 52 cm.

Publisher: Galerie Berggruen, Paris.
Printer: Mourlot, Paris.

BIBLIOGRAPHY:

Catalogue for the Exhibition "Joan Miró. Le lézard aux plumes d'or". Galerie Berggruen, Paris, 1971.
HERRMANNS, Ralph: *Affischer av Miró*. A.H. Grafik, Stockholm, 1974, page 69, No. 53.
Catalogue for the Exhibition "Miró, l'œuvre graphique". Musée d'Art Moderne de la Ville de Paris, 1974, page 142, No. 573.

JOAN MIRÓ

Louis Broder Éditeur

GALERIE BERGGRUEN

70 rue de l'Université, Paris VII — du 23 novembre au 31 décembre 1971

MOURLOT

54. "QÜESTIONS D'ART". 1971.

Poster produced by Miró for the presentation in Barcelona of the magazine "Qüestions d'Art".
This drawing was published on the cover of No. 17 of this magazine in 1971.

Publication:
Indefinite number of copies on standard paper.
Size: 69 × 48 cm.

Publisher: Qüestions d'Art, Barcelona.
Printer: Grafesa, Barcelona.

QÜESTIONS D'ART

LA REVISTA CATALANA D'ART ACTUAL · LA REVISTA CATALANA D'ART ACTUAL · LA REVISTA CATALANA D'ART
DEMANEU INFORMACIO AQUI I A: Q.Ü.A. PROVENÇA 273 · BARCELONA-8 · DEMANEU INFORMACIO AQUI

55. "HOMENAJE A JOSEP-LLUÍS SERT" EXHIBITION. 1972.

Poster produced by Miró for the exhibition in homage to the architect Josep-Lluís Sert, held at the Colegio de Arquitectos de Canarias, Santa Cruz de Tenerife (February 1972).

Publication:
1,000 copies on standard paper.
Size: 75 × 58 cm.

150 copies *avant la lettre* on Guarro paper, numbered and signed.
50 copies *avant la lettre* in black, on Guarro paper, numbered and signed.
Printing process: colour lithographic press.
Size: 75 × 58 cm.

Publisher: Colegio de Arquitectos de Canarias, Santa Cruz de Tenerife.
Printer: La Polígrafa, S.A., Barcelona.

BIBLIOGRAPHY:

HERRMANNS, Ralph: *Affischer av Miró*. A.H. Grafik, Stockholm, 1974, page 69, No. 45.
Catalogue for the Exhibition "Joan Miró. Obra Gráfica". Halls of the Dirección General del Patrimonio Artístico, Archivos y Museos, Madrid, 1978, pages 82-83, No. 227.
Catalogue for the Exhibition "Joan Miró. Grafica". Palazzo Pubblico, Siena, 1979, page 72, page 91, No. 221.

EXPOSICION HOMENAJE A JOSEP·LLUÍS SERT
COLEGIO DE ARQUITECTOS DE CANARIAS

SANTA CRUZ DE TENERIFE · FEBRERO 1972

LA POLIGRAFA S. A. BARCELONA. PRINTED IN SPAIN   DEP. LEGAL B. 410/972

56. "HOMENATGE A JOAN PRATS" EXHIBITION. 1972.

Poster produced for the presentation of the series of 15 lithographs *Homenatge a Joan Prats* by Miró, published by Ed. Polígrafa, S.A., at the Galerie Berggruen, Paris (February 1972).

This poster was later used for the presentation of this series of lithographs at the Galerie Pierre, Stockholm (4 December 1971 to 25 January 1972).

Publication:
1,000 copies on standard paper.
Size: 75.5 × 56 cm.

150 copies *avant la lettre* on Guarro paper, numbered and signed.
Printing process: colour lithographic press.
Size: 75.5 × 56 cm.

Publisher: Galerie Berggruen, Paris.
Printer: La Polígrafa, S.A., Barcelona.

BIBLIOGRAPHY:

HERRMANNS, Ralph: *Affischer av Miró*. A.H. Grafik, Stockholm, 1974, page 69, No. 49.
Catalogue for the Exhibition "Miró, l'œuvre graphique". Musée d'Art Moderne de la Ville de Paris, 1974, page 142, No. 574.

BERGGRUEN

70, RUE DE L'UNIVERSITÉ · PARIS · FEVRIER 1972

HOMMAGE À JOAN PRATS : 15 Lithographies originales de Joan Miró.

LA POLIGRAFA, S. A. BARCELONA PRINTED IN SPAIN

DEP. LEGAL. B. 2438-1971

57. "MIRÓ BRONZES" EXHIBITION. 1972.

Poster produced for the exhibition of 51 Miró sculptures at the Hayward Gallery, London (2 February to 12 March 1972).

Publication:
Indefinite number of copies on standard paper.
Size: 90 × 56 cm.
There are reprints of this poster.

150 copies *avant la lettre* on Arches paper, numbered and signed.
Printing process: colour lithographic press.
Size: 88.5 × 62 cm.

Publisher: Arts Council, London.
Printer: Arte Adrien Maeght, Paris.

BIBLIOGRAPHY:

HERRMANNS, Ralph: *Affischer av Miró.* A.H. Grafik, Stockholm, 1974, page 70, No. 55.
Catalogue for the Exhibition "Miró, l'œuvre graphique". Musée d'Art Moderne de la Ville de Paris, 1974, page 143, page 145, No. 576.
Catalogue for the Exhibition "Joan Miró. Obra Gráfica". Halls of the Dirección General del Patrimonio Artístico, Archivos y Museos, Madrid, 1978, page 82, page 84, No. 228.
Catalogue for the Exhibition "Joan Miró. Grafica". Palazzo Pubblico, Siena, 1979, page 73, page 91, No. 222.

BRONZES

HAYWARD GALLERY
2 FEBRUARY -
12 MARCH 1972
AN ARTS COUNCIL
EXHIBITION

MONDAYS WEDNESDAYS
FRIDAYS SATURDAYS 10-6
TUESDAYS
AND THURSDAYS 10-8
SUNDAYS 12-6

ADMISSION 30P
TUESDAYS
AND THURSDAYS 5-8
ADMISSION 10P
(ADMITS ALSO
TO RIETVELD
AND ROTHKO
EXHIBITIONS)

58. "SOBRETEIXIMS I ESCULTURES" EXHIBITION. 1972.

Poster produced for the Miró exhibition *Sobreteixims i escultures* at the Sala Gaspar, Barcelona (16 May to June 1972).

This poster was later used for the retrospective Miró exhibition at the Liljevalchs Kunsthalle, Stockholm (October 1972), and also for the Miró graphic work exhibition at the Tel-Aviv Art Museum (June-July 1973).

Publication:
1,000 copies on standard paper.
Size: 85.5 × 56 cm.

150 copies *avant la lettre* on Guarro paper, numbered and signed.
Printing process: colour lithographic press.
Size: 85.5 × 56 cm.

Publisher: Sala Gaspar, Barcelona.
Printer: Publicaciones Reunidas, S.A., Barcelona.

BIBLIOGRAPHY:

HERRMANNS, Ralph: *Affischer av Miró*. A.H. Grafik, Stockholm, 1974, page 62, No. 23.
Catalogue for the Exhibition "Miró, l'œuvre graphique". Musée d'Art Moderne de la Ville de Paris, 1974, page 143, No. 580.

SALA GASPAR

SOBRETEIXIMS I ESCULTURES

BARCELONA - MAIG - 1972

59. "PEINTURES, GOUACHES, DESSINS" EXHIBITION. 1972.

Poster produced for the exhibition of 72 Miró works — paintings, gouaches and drawings — at the Galerie Maeght, Zürich (June-July 1972).

Publication:
Indefinite number of copies on standard paper.
Size: 74 × 34.5 cm.

150 copies *avant la lettre* on Arches paper, numbered and signed.
Printing process: colour lithographic press.
Size: 77 × 37.5 cm.

Publisher: Galerie Maeght, Zürich.
Printer: Arte Adrien Maeght, Paris.

BIBLIOGRAPHY:

HERRMANNS, Ralph: *Affischer av Miró*. A.H. Grafik, Stockholm, 1974, page 59, No. 22.
Catalogue for the Exhibition "Miró, l'œuvre graphique". Musée d'Art Moderne de la Ville de Paris, 1974, page 143, No. 577.

MAEGHT·ZÜRICH

PREDIGERPLATZ 10–12 · TELEFON 01 321120–321387

JUNI–JULI 1972

60. "DAS PLASTISCHE WERK" EXHIBITION. 1972.

Poster produced for the exhibition of 194 works by Miró at the Kunsthaus, Zürich (4 June to 30 July 1972).

This lithograph is a variation on the one used for the poster advertising the exhibition "Miró Bronzes" in 1972, which has been turned upside down.

Publication:
Indefinite number of copies on standard paper.
Size: 90×56 cm., placed on a support 128×90 cm.

Publisher: Kunsthaus, Zürich.
Printer: Arte Adrien Maeght, Paris.

BIBLIOGRAPHY:

HERRMANNS, Ralph: *Affischer av Miró*. A.H. Grafik, Stockholm, 1974, page 70, No. 56.
Catalogue for the Exhibition "Miró, l'œuvre graphique". Musée d'Art Moderne de la Ville de Paris, 1974, page 143, No. 579.

Joan Miró
Das plastische Werk

4. Juni bis 30. Juli 1972

Dienstag bis Freitag 10 – 17 und 20 – 22 Uhr
Samstag und Sonntag 10 – 17 Uhr
Montag nur 14 – 17 Uhr

Kunsthaus Zürich

61. "HOMENATGE A JOSEP-LLUÍS SERT I JOSEP LLORENS
    ARTIGAS" EXHIBITION. 1972.

Poster produced by Miró with a collage of photographs by the photographer
Català-Roca, for the exhibition in homage to the architect Josep-Lluís Sert and the
ceramist Josep Llorens Artigas, at the Colegio de Arquitectos de Cataluña y
Baleares, Barcelona (November-December 1972).

Publication:
1,000 copies on standard paper.
Size: 69.5 × 47 cm.

Publisher: Colegio de Arquitectos de Cataluña y Baleares, Barcelona.
Printer: La Polígrafa, S.A., Barcelona.

HOMENATGE

JOSEP

JOSEP LLUÍS SERT i

LLORENS ARTIGAS

miró

COLEGIO DE ARQUITECTOS DE CATALUÑA Y BALEARES, PLAZA NUEVA, 5 - NOVIEMBRE-DICIEMBRE 1972

LA POLIGRAFA, S. A. Balmes, 54. BARCELONA · FOTOS: F. CATALA ROCA   DEP. LEGAL. B. 46.364 - 1972

62. "DAS GRAPHISCHE WERK" EXHIBITION. 1973.

Poster for the exhibition of Miró's graphic work at the Kunstverein, Hamburg, and of original posters at the Haus Deutscher Ring, in the same city (31 March to 24 April 1973).

There are two versions of this poster, one in which only the exhibition of graphic work in the Kunstverein is mentioned and the other of 100 copies in which the exhibition of original posters is also mentioned.

This poster was later used for Miró's exhibition at the Galerie Dürr, Munich (June 1973).

Publication:
2,000 copies on standard paper.
Size: 73 × 50 cm.

1,000 copies *avant la lettre* on Arches paper, numbered and signed.
Size: 75.5 × 55.5 cm.

Publisher: Kunstverein, Hamburg.
Printer: Arte Adrien Maeght, Paris.

BIBLIOGRAPHY:

HERRMANNS, Ralph: *Affischer av Miró*. A.H. Grafik, Stockholm, 1974, page 70, No. 57.
Catalogue for the Exhibition "Miró, l'œuvre graphique". Musée d'Art Moderne de la Ville de Paris, 1974, page 143, No. 581.
"Art News", New York, Vol. 78, No. 9, November 1979, page 129.

KUNSTVEREIN IN HAMBURG
DAS GRAPHISCHE WERK
31 MÄRZ - 29 APRIL 1973
TÄGL 10-18,
MITTWOCHS 10-20,
MONTAGS GESCHLOSSEN

7. Ausstellung
im Haus Deutscher **Ring**

Joan Miró
Original-
Plakate

2 Hamburg 11, Ost-West-Straße 110 (gegenüber dem Michel)
6. April bis 29. April 1973

IMPRIMERIE ARTE PARIS

63. "SÈRIE MALLORCA" EXHIBITION. 1973.

Poster produced for the presentation of the series of nine etchings called *Sèrie Mallorca,* produced by Miró and published by Sala Pelaires, Palma de Mallorca; the exhibition was held at the Sala Pelaires (April 1973).

This poster was later used for the presentation of this series of etchings at the Artes Galleri, Oslo (November-December 1973), at the Galería Studium, Valladolid (October-November 1973) and at the Galeria Adrià, Barcelona (12 December 1973 to 5 January 1974).

Publication:
1,000 copies on standard paper
Size: 75 × 55 cm.

75 copies *avant la lettre* on Guarro paper, numbered and signed.
Printing process: colour silk-screen print.
Size: 79 × 64 cm.

Publisher: Sala Pelaires, Palma de Mallorca.
Printer: La Polígrafa, S.A., Barcelona.

BIBLIOGRAPHY:

HERRMANNS, Ralph: *Affischer av Miró.* A.H. Grafik, Stockholm, 1974, page 70, No. 60.
Catalogue for the Exhibition "Miró, l'œuvre graphique". Musée d'Art Moderne de la Ville de Paris, 1974, page 143, No. 585.

64. "SOBRETEIXIMS" EXHIBITION. 1973.

Poster produced for the exhibition "Sobreteixims" by Miró at the Galerie Maeght, Paris (10 April to May 1973).

Publication:
Indefinite number of copies on standard paper.
Size: 83.5 × 56 cm.
       160 × 120 cm.

450 copies *avant la lettre* on Chiffon de la Dore paper, numbered and signed.
Size: 88 × 63 cm.
40 copies *avant la lettre* on special paper, numbered and signed.
Size: 151 × 119 cm.
Printing process: colour lithographic press.

Publisher: Galerie Maeght, Paris.
Printer: Arte Adrien Maeght, Paris.

BIBLIOGRAPHY:

HERRMANNS, Ralph: *Affischer av Miró*. A.H. Grafik, Stockholm, 1974, page 70, No. 58.
Catalogue for the Exhibition "Miró, l'œuvre graphique". Musée d'Art Moderne de la Ville de Paris, 1974, page 143, Nos. 582 and 583.
Catalogue for the Exhibition "Affiches-Posters 1979". Maeght Ed., Paris, 1979, No. 137.

GALERIE MAEGHT

65. "SCULPTURES ET CÉRAMIQUES" EXHIBITION. 1973.

Poster produced for the exhibition of 278 works — sculptures by Miró and ceramics by Miró and Llorens Artigas — at the Maeght Foundation, Saint-Paul-de-Vence (14 April to 30 June 1973).

Publication:
Indefinite number of copies on standard paper.
Size: 83 × 56 cm.

150 copies *avant la lettre* on Arches paper, numbered and signed.
Printing process: colour lithographic press.
Size: 86 × 59 cm.

Publisher: Fondation Maeght, Saint-Paul-de-Vence.
Printer: Arte Adrien Maeght, Paris.

BIBLIOGRAPHY:

HERRMANNS, Ralph: *Affischer av Miró*. A.H. Grafik, Stockholm, 1974, page 70, No. 59.
Catalogue for the Exhibition "Miró, l'œuvre graphique". Musée d'Art Moderne de la Ville de Paris, 1974, page 143, No. 584.
Catalogue "Affiches - Posters 1979". Maeght Ed., Paris, 1979.

FONDATION MAEGHT
06 SAINT-PAUL - DU 14 AVRIL AU 30 JUIN 1973
SCULPTURES ET CERAMIQUES

66. "KRISTIANSTADS MUSEUM" EXHIBITION. 1973.

Poster produced for the exhibition of Miró's posters at the Art Museum, Kristianstad, Sweden (7 June to 10 September 1973).

Publication:
900 copies on standard paper, numbered.
Size: 70 × 51 cm.

400 copies *avant la lettre* on Schoeller paper, numbered from I/CD to CD/CD.
Size: 101 × 70.5 cm.
75 copies *avant la lettre* on Schoeller paper, numbered and signed.
Size: 74.5 × 56 cm.
Printing process: colour silk-screen print.

Publisher: Société des Admirateurs de Joan Miró.
Printer: Sala Pelaires, Palma de Mallorca.

BIBLIOGRAPHY:

HERRMANNS, Ralph: *Affischer av Miró*. A.H. Grafik, Stockholm, 1974, page 63, No. 24.
Catalogue for the Exhibition "Miró, l'œuvre graphique". Musée d'Art Moderne de la Ville de Paris, 1974, page 143, No. 587.
JOHANSSON, Kjell A.: *Miró en Escania*. "Dagens Nyheter", Stockholm, 30 June 1976.

KRISTIANSTADS
MUSEUM

SOCIÉTÉ DES
ADMIRATEURS
DE JOAN MIRÓ

7/VI - 10/IX 1973

765   900

67. "SCULPTURES EN MONTAGNE" EXHIBITION. 1973.

Poster produced by Miró for the collective sculpture exhibition in Passy-Plateau-d'Assy, France (15 June to 30 September 1973).

Publication:
Indefinite number of copies on standard paper.
Size: 86 × 55 cm.

150 copies *avant la lettre* on Arches paper, numbered and signed.
Printing process: colour lithographic press.
Size: 77.5 × 55 cm.

Publisher: Sculptures en Montagne, Passy.
Printer: Arte Adrien Maeght, Paris.

BIBLIOGRAPHY:

HERRMANNS, Ralph: *Affischer av Miró*. A.H. Grafik, Stockholm, 1974, page 71, No. 64.
Catalogue for the Exhibition "Miró, l'œuvre graphique". Musée d'Art Moderne de la Ville de Paris, 1974, page 147, No. 594.

SCULPTURES EN MONTAGNE
poème dans l'espace
AU PAYS DU MONT-BLANC
PASSY-PLATEAU D'ASSY . 74, FRANCE
du 15 juin au 30 septembre 1973

avec   calder   gilioli   •   muller

cardenas   guino   otero

casadesus   guzman   patkaï

chavignier   hernandez   roussil

delfino   kijno   schultze

feraud   lemesle   semser

étienne martin   miró   singer

gardy artigas   mizui   van thienen

68. "ŒUVRE GRAVÉ ORIGINAL" EXHIBITION. 1973.

Poster produced by Miró for the exhibition of graphic work by Max Ernst, Jacques Villon and Miró himself, at the Musée de l'Athénée, Geneva (4 July to 22 December 1973).

For the production of this poster Miró used the same lithographic black stone as for the poster *Das graphische Werk* (1973), turning it upside down and modifying some of the colours.

Publication:
Indefinite number of copies on standard paper.
Size: 76 × 50 cm.

75 copies *avant la lettre* on Arches paper, numbered and signed.
Printing process: colour lithographic press.
Size: 76 × 55.6 cm.

Publisher: Musée de l'Athénée, Geneva.
Printer: Arte Adrien Maeght, Paris.

BIBLIOGRAPHY:

HERRMANNS, Ralph: *Affischer av Miró*. A.H. Grafik, Stockholm, 1974, page 71, No. 65.
Catalogue for the Exhibition "Miró, l'œuvre graphique", Musée d'Art Moderne de la Ville de Paris, page 143, No. 586.
"Art News", New York, Vol. 78, No. 5, May 1979, page 123.

ŒUVRE GRAVÉ ORIGINAL

MUSÉE DE L'ATHÉNÉE GENÈVE

DU 4 JUILLET AU 22 DÉCEMBRE 1973

tous les jours de 10 h à midi et de 14 h à 18 h, le samedi jusqu'à 17 h,
le dimanche matin de 10 h à midi et le mardi soir de 20 à 22 h,
fermé le lundi matin.

ARTE - PARIS

69. "LIVRES ILLUSTRÉS ET LITHOGRAPHIES" EXHIBITION. 1973.

Poster for the exhibition of books illustrated by Miró and lithographs produced by him at the Galerie Gérald Cramer, Geneva (16 October to 10 November 1973).

Publication:
2,000 copies on standard paper.
Size: 65 × 50 cm.

100 copies *avant la lettre* on Rives paper, numbered and signed.
Printing process: colour lithographic press.
Size: 65 × 50 cm.

Publisher: Galerie Gérald Cramer, Geneva.
Printer: La Polígrafa, S.A., Barcelona.

BIBLIOGRAPHY:

Catalogue for the Exhibition "Joan Miró, Livres illustrés et lithographies". Galerie Gérald Cramer, Geneva, 1973, front cover.
Catalogue for the Exhibition "Miró, l'œuvre graphique". Musée d'Art Moderne de la Ville de Paris, 1974, page 143, No. 588.

GALERIE GÉRALD CRAMER

13 RUE DE CHANTEPOULET · GENÈVE

16 OCTOBRE · 10 NOVEMBRE 1973

LIVRES ILLUSTRÉS ET LITHOGRAPHIES

LA POLIGRAFA, S. A. · BARCELONA · PRINTED IN SPAIN

DEP. LEGAL B 38954-1973

70. "HOMAGE TO MIRÓ" EXHIBITION. 1973.

Poster for the exhibition of Miró's painting, sculptures and drawings at the Museum of Modern Art, New York (10 October to December 1973).

Publication:
5,000 copies on standard paper.
Size: 90 × 61 cm.

150 copies *avant la lettre* on Arches paper, numbered and signed.
Printing process: colour lithographic press.
Size: 90 × 61 cm.

Publisher: Museum of Modern Art, New York.
Printer: Arte Adrien Maeght, Paris.

BIBLIOGRAPHY:

Catalogue for the Exhibition "Miró, l'œuvre graphique". Musée d'Art Moderne de la Ville de Paris, 1974, page 143, No. 589.
Catalogue for the Exhibition "Joan Miró. Obra Gráfica". Halls of the Dirección General del Patrimonio Artístico, Archivos y Museos, Madrid, 1978, page 82, No. 229.
Catalogue for the Exhibition "Joan Miró. Grafica". Palazzo Pubblico, Siena, 1979, page 91, No. 223.

HOMAGE TO MIRÓ

PAINTINGS, SCULPTURE, DRAWINGS IN THE COLLECTION OF

THE MUSEUM OF MODERN ART, NEW YORK

OCTOBER 10 - DECEMBER 10, 1973

Imprimerie Arte. Paris - Printed in France

71. "UNIVERSITÉ DE GENÈVE". 1973.

Poster produced by Miró for the International Culture Centre of Geneva University.

Publication:
Indefinite number of copies on standard paper.
Size: 61 × 49 cm.

50 copies *avant la lettre* on Arches paper, numbered and signed.
Printing process: colour lithographic press.
Size: 38 × 31 cm.

Publisher: Université de Genève, Geneva.
Printer: Mourlot, Paris.

BIBLIOGRAPHY:

Catalogue for the Exhibition "Miró, l'œuvre graphique". Musée d'Art Moderne de la Ville de Paris, 1974, page 143, No. 593.

UNIVERSITÉ DE GENÈVE

CENTRE CULTUREL
INTERNATIONAL

72. "MALLORCA". 1973.

Poster produced by Miró, commissioned by the *Fomento de Turismo Español,* to promote the island of Mallorca.

Publication:
100,000 copies on standard paper.
Size: 99 × 68.5 cm.

Publisher: Consejo del Fomento de Turismo, Palma de Mallorca.
Printer: La Polígrafa, S.A., Barcelona.

BIBLIOGRAPHY:

"La Vanguardia Española", Barcelona, 9 August 1973.
HERRMANNS, Ralph: *Affischer av Miró.* A.H. Grafik, Stockholm, 1974, page 71, No. 66.
Catalogue for the Exhibition "Miró, l'œuvre graphique". Musée d'Art Moderne de la Ville de Paris, 1974, page 147, No. 596.
Arte español 77. Ed. Lápiz, Madrid, 1977, page 176.
Catalogue for the Exhibition "Joan Miró. Obra Gráfica". Halls of the Dirección General del Patrimonio Artístico, Archivos y Museos, Madrid, 1978, page 82, No. 231.
Catalogue for the Exhibition "Joan Miró. Grafica". Palazzo Pubblico, Siena, 1979, page 91, No. 226.

Es un consejo
del Fomento de Turismo

Visite nuestra isla

73. "YOUNG ARTISTS '73" EXHIBITION. 1973.

Poster produced by Miró for the exhibition "Young Artists '73" in New York and Saratoga Springs.

Publication:
5,000 copies on standard paper.
Size: 90 × 61 cm.

75 copies *avant la lettre* on Arches paper, numbered and signed.
Printing process: colour lithographic press.
Size: 90 × 61 cm.

Publisher: International Play Group, New York.
Printer: Arte Adrien Maeght, Paris.

BIBLIOGRAPHY:

Catalogue for the Exhibition "Miró, l'œuvre graphique". Musée d'Art Moderne de la Ville de Paris, 1974, page 143, No. 592.
Catalogue for the Exhibition "Joan Miró. Grafica". Palazzo Pubblico, Siena, 1979, page 91, No. 225.

YOUNG ARTISTS, '73

NEW YORK CITY . SARATOGA SPRINGS

74. "UMBRACLE". 1973.

Poster produced by Miró for the presentation of Pere Portabella's film *Umbracle*.

Publication:
500 copies on standard paper.
Size: 74.5 × 56 cm.

50 copies *avant la lettre* on special Sala Gaspar paper, numbered and signed.
Printing process: colour lithographic press.
Size: 74.5 × 56 cm.

Publisher: Pere Portabella, Barcelona.
Printer: Puresa, Barcelona.

BIBLIOGRAPHY:

HERRMANNS, Ralph: *Affischer av Miró*. A.H. Grafik, Stockholm, 1974, page 71, No. 62.
Catalogue for the Exhibition "Miró, l'œuvre graphique". Musée d'Art Moderne de la Ville de Paris, 1974, page 143, No. 590.

Un film de

PERE PORTABELLA

Amb CHRISTOPHER LEE i JANINE MESTRES — Guió: JOAN BROSSA i PERE PORTABELLA

Banda sonora: CARLES SANTOS — Fotografia: MANEL ESTEBAN

FILMS-59

75. "PER UN TEATRE A CATALUNYA". 1973.

Poster produced by Miró in support of theatre in Catalonia.

Publication:
The poster could not be run off on standard paper.

50 copies *avant la lettre* on special Sala Gaspar paper, numbered and signed.
Printing process: colour lithographic press.
Size: 75 × 56 cm.

Publisher: Sala Gaspar, Barcelona.
Printer: Puresa, Barcelona.

BIBLIOGRAPHY:

HERRMANNS, Ralph: *Affischer av Miró*. A. H. Grafik, Stockholm, 1974, page 71, No. 63.
Catalogue for the Exhibition "Miró, l'œuvre graphique". Musée d'Art Moderne de la Ville de Paris, 1974, page 143, No. 591.
"Avui", Barcelona, 20 April 1978, page 14.
Catalogue for the Exhibition "Joan Miró. Grafica". Palazzo Pubblico, Siena, 1979, page 91, No. 224.

76. "MIRÓ-GRAND PALAIS" EXHIBITION. 1974.

Poster for the retrospective exhibition of Miró's painting and sculpture at the Grand Palais, Paris (18 May to 13 October 1974).

Publication:
Indefinite number of copies on standard paper.
Size: 60 × 40 cm.

100 copies *avant la lettre* on Arches paper, numbered and signed.
Printing process: colour lithographic press.
Size: 65 × 52 cm.

Publisher: Réunion des Musées Nationaux, Paris.
Printer: Arte Adrien Maeght, Paris.

BIBLIOGRAPHY:

Catalogue for the Exhibition "Miró, l'œuvre graphique". Musée d'Art Moderne de la Ville de Paris, 1974, page 147, No. 597.
Catalogue for the Exhibition "Joan Miró". Exhibition Room of the Caixa d'Estalvis i Mont de Pietat de Barcelona, Manresa (Barcelona), 1977, No. 58.
Catalogue for the Exhibition "Joan Miró. Obra Gráfica". Halls of the Dirección General del Patrimonio Artístico, Archivos y Museos, Madrid, 1978, page 82, No. 232.
Catalogue for the Exhibition "Joan Miró. Obra gràfica". Exhibition Room of the Caixa d'Estalvis Laietana, Mataró (Barcelona), 1978, No. 13.

**Grand Palais
18 mai -
13 octobre
1974**

**ouvert
tous les jours
sauf
le mardi
de 10 à 20 h
le mercredi
jusqu'à 22 h**

Joan Miró

77. "MIRÓ-GRAND PALAIS" EXHIBITION. 1974.

Large-scale poster for the retrospective exhibition of Miró's painting and sculpture at the Grand Palais, Paris (18 May to 13 October 1974).

Publication:
Indefinite number of copies on standard paper.
Size: 160 × 120 cm.

50 copies *avant la lettre* on Arches paper, numbered and signed.
Printing process: colour lithographic press.
Size: 157 × 118.5 cm.

Publisher: Réunion des Musées Nationaux, Paris.
Printer: Arte Adrien Maeght, Paris.

BIBLIOGRAPHY:

Catalogue for the Exhibition "Miró, l'œuvre graphique". Musée d'Art Moderne de la Ville de Paris, 1974, page 147, No. 598.
Catalogue for the Exhibition "Joan Miró. Obra Gráfica". Halls of the Dirección General del Patrimonio Artístico, Archivos y Museos, Madrid, 1978, page 85, No. 233.

Grand Palais 18 mai–
13 octobre
1974

Joan Miró

78. "MIRÓ, L'ŒUVRE GRAPHIQUE" EXHIBITION. 1974.

Poster for the retrospective exhibition of graphic work, illustrations for books and posters by Miró at the Musée d'Art Moderne de la Ville de Paris (22 May to 15 September 1974).

Publication:
Indefinite number of copies on standard paper.
Size: 73.5 × 54.5 cm.

100 copies *avant la lettre* on Arches paper, numbered and signed.
Printing process: colour lithographic press.
Size: 78 × 57 cm.

Publisher: Musée d'Art Moderne de la Ville de Paris.
Printer: Arte Adrien Maeght, Paris.

BIBLIOGRAPHY:

Catalogue for the Exhibition "Joan Miró". Exhibition Room of the Caixa d'Estalvis i Mont de Pietat de Barcelona, Manresa (Barcelona), 1977, No. 59.
Catalogue for the Exhibition "Joan Miró. Obra gràfica". Exhibition Room of the Caixa d'Estalvis Laietana, Mataró (Barcelona), 1978, No. 14.

miró

l'œuvre graphique

MUSÉE D'ART MODERNE DE LA VILLE DE PARIS
AVENUE DU PRESIDENT WILSON _ 22 MAI / 15 SEPTEMBRE 1974
OUVERT TOUS LES JOURS DE 10 H A 17 H 45 SAUF LE SAMEDI ET LE MARDI

79. OPENING OF THE GALERIA MAEGHT-BARCELONA EXHIBITION. 1974.

Poster produced by Miró for the group show held to mark the opening of the Galeria Maeght, Barcelona (November-December 1974).

Publication:
1,300 copies on standard paper.
Size: 65.5 × 40 cm.

75 copies *avant la lettre* on Guarro paper, numbered and signed.
Printing process: colour lithographic press.
Size: 69 × 52.5 cm.

Publisher: Galeria Maeght, Barcelona.
Printer: Litografías Artísticas Damià Caus, Barcelona.

BIBLIOGRAPHY:

CLEMENTE, Josep Carles: *Miró invade las calles de Barcelona*. "Gaceta del Arte", Madrid, Year III, No. 35, 15 January 1975, page 4.

galeria maeght
exposició inaugural
novembre desembre 1974
carrer montcada 25 barcelona

80. "OBRA GRÁFICA-FUNDAÇÃO GULBENKIAN"
EXHIBITION. 1974.

Poster produced for the retrospective exhibition of Miró's graphic work at the Gulbenkian Foundation, Lisbon (25 November to 31 December 1974).

Publication:
3,000 copies on standard paper.
Size: 68 × 50 cm.

75 copies *avant la lettre* on Arches paper, numbered and signed.
Printing process: colour lithographic press.
Size: 75 × 55 cm.

Publisher: Gulbenkian Foundation, Lisbon.
Printer: Arte Adrien Maeght, Paris.

obra gráfica
FUNDAÇÃO CALOUSTE GULBENKIAN
LISBOA - 25 NOVEMBRO 31 DEZEMBRO 1974

81. "ÒMNIUM CULTURAL". 1974.

Poster produced by Miró for the Catalan cultural association *Òmnium Cultural,* Barcelona.

Publication:
2,000 copies on standard paper.
Size: 73 × 54 cm.

75 copies *avant la lettre* on Guarro paper, numbered and signed.
Printing process: colour lithographic press.
Size: 73 × 54 cm.

Publisher: Òmnium Cultural, Barcelona.
Printer: La Polígrafa, S.A., Barcelona.

BIBLIOGRAPHY:

Catalogue for the Exhibition "Miró, l'œuvre graphique". Musée d'Art Moderne de la Ville de Paris, 1974, page 147, No. 595.
"Diario de Barcelona", Barcelona, 23 June 1974.
CLEMENTE, Josep Carles: *Miró invade las calles de Barcelona.* "Gaceta del Arte", Madrid, Year II, No. 35, 15 January 1975, page 4.
Catalogue for the Exhibition "Joan Miró. Obra Gráfica". Halls of the Dirección General del Patrimonio Artístico, Archivos y Museos, Madrid, 1978, page 82, No. 230.
Catalogue for the Exhibition "Joan Miró. Grafica". Palazzo Pubblico, Siena, 1979, page 91, No. 227.

ÒMNIUM CULTURAL

82. "FUTBOL CLUB BARCELONA". 1974

Poster produced by Miró for the 75th anniversary of Barcelona Football Club.

Publication:
50,000 copies on standard paper.
Size: 99×68.5 cm.

50 copies *avant la lettre* on Guarro paper, signed.
Printing process: colour offset.
Size: 99×68.5 cm.

Publisher: Futbol Club Barcelona, Barcelona.
Printer: La Polígrafa, S.A., Barcelona.

BIBLIOGRAPHY:

"Tele-Exprés", Barcelona, 2 April 1974.
"La Vanguardia Española", Barcelona, 12 May 1974.
"El Correo Catalán", Barcelona, 29 November 1974.
Catalogue for the Exhibition "Miró, l'œuvre graphique". Musée d'Art Moderne de la Ville de Paris, 1974, page 147, No. 599.
CLEMENTE, Josep Carles: *Miró invade las calles de Barcelona.* "Gaceta del Arte", Madrid, Year III, No. 35, 15 January 1975, page 4.
JOHANSSON, Kjell A.: *Miró en Escania.* "Dagens Nyheter", Stockholm, 30 June 1976.
RAILLARD, Georges: *Joan Miró. Ceci est la couleur de mes rêves.* Ed. du Seuil, Paris, 1977, page 17.
"Avui", Barcelona, 20 April 1978.
Catalogue for the Exhibition "Joan Miró. Obra Gráfica". Halls of the Dirección General del Patrimonio Artístico, Archivos y Museos, Madrid, 1978, page 85, No. 234.
Catalogue for the Exhibition "Joan Miró. Obra gràfica". Exhibition Room of the Caixa d'Estalvis Laietana, Mataró (Barcelona), 1978, No. 31.
CALVET MATA, Rossend: *Historia del Futbol Club Barcelona.* Ed. Hispano Europea, Barcelona, 1978, front cover.
Catalogue for the Exhibition "Joan Miró. Grafica". Palazzo Pubblico, Siena, 1979, page 91, No. 228.

FUTBOL CLUB BARCELONA

75 Aniversari (1899·1974)

83. "UNESCO-DROITS DE L'HOMME", 1974.

Poster produced by Miró in support of the Human Rights campaign by Unesco. This poster was published with Spanish and English texts.

Publication:
5,500 copies on standard paper.
Size: 74 × 54.5 cm.

75 copies *avant la lettre* on Arches paper, numbered and signed.
Printing process: colour lithographic press.
Size: 80 × 60 cm.

Publisher: Unesco, Paris.
Printer: Arte Adrien Maeght, Paris.

BIBLIOGRAPHY:

Catalogue for the Exhibition "Joan Miró. Obra gràfica". Exhibition Room of the Caixa d'Estalvis Laietana, Mataró (Barcelona), 1978, No. 37.
"Art News", New York, Vol. 79, No. 3, March 1980, page 113.

unesco   miró

droits de l'homme

84. "LOUISIANA" EXHIBITION. 1974.

Poster for the exhibition of Miró's paintings, drawings, sculptures and graphic work at the Louisiana Modern Art Museum, Humleback, Denmark (9 November 1974 to 13 January 1975).

Publication:
Indefinite number of copies on standard paper.
Size: 65.5 × 49 cm.

75 copies *avant la lettre* on Arches paper, numbered and signed.
Printing process: colour lithographic press.
Size: 70 × 55 cm.

Publisher: Louisiana Modern Art Museum, Humleback.
Printer: Arte Adrien Maeght, Paris.

louisiana

9.11.74 - 13.1.75

85. OPENING OF THE FUNDACIÓ JOAN MIRÓ. 1975.

Poster for the opening of the Fundació Joan Miró, Centre d'Estudis d'Art Contemporani, in Barcelona (10 June 1975).

Publication:
2,000 copies on standard paper.
Size: 70 × 50 cm.

99 copies *avant la lettre* on Guarro paper, numbered and signed.
Printing process: colour lithographic press.
Size: 70 × 50 cm.

Publisher: Fundació Joan Miró, Barcelona.
Printer: La Polígrafa, S.A., Barcelona.

BIBLIOGRAPHY:

Catalogue for the Exhibition "Joan Miró. Obra Gráfica". Halls of the Dirección General del Patrimonio Artístico, Archivos y Museos, Madrid, 1978, page 85, No. 239.
Catalogue for the Exhibition "Joan Miró. Obra gràfica". Exhibition Room of the Caixa d'Estalvis Laietana, Mataró (Barcelona), 1978, No. 37.

FUNDACIÓ JOAN MIRÓ
Centre d'Estudis d'Art Contemporani

Parc de Montjuïc   **BARCELONA**
Obertura, 10 de juny del 1975

Hores de visita: Cada dia de les onze del matí a les vuit del vespre   (exceptuant els dilluns)

86. "LUCIFER". 1975.

Poster produced by Miró for the presentation of the ballet *Lucifer* by the Martha Graham Dance Company, at the Uris Theater, New York (June 1975).

Publication:
5,000 copies on standard paper.
Size: 80 × 53.5 cm.

75 copies *avant la lettre* on Arches paper, numbered and signed.
Printing process: colour lithographic press.
Size: 78 × 56.5 cm.

Publisher: Galerie Maeght, Paris.
Printer: Arte Adrien Maeght, Paris.

MARGOT FONTEYN and RUDOLF NUREYEV
in LUCIFER
by MARTHA GRAHAM

WITH MARTHA GRAHAM DANCE COMPANY

June 1975   Uris Theater   New York City

87. "UN CAMÍ COMPARTIT (MIRÓ-MAEGHT)" EXHIBITION. 1975.

Poster produced for Miró's exhibition "Un Camí compartit" at the Galeria Maeght, Barcelona (5 December 1975 to 31 January 1976).

Publication:
900 copies on standard paper.
Size: 75 × 54.5 cm.

75 copies *avant la lettre* on Arches paper, numbered and signed.
Printing process: colour lithographic press.
Size: 73 × 54 cm.

Publisher: Galeria Maeght, Barcelona.
Printer: Litografías Artísticas Damià Caus, Barcelona.

BIBLIOGRAPHY:

"La Vanguardia Española", Barcelona, 4 January 1976.
RAILLARD, Georges: *"Joan Miró. Ceci est la couleur de mes rêves"*. Ed. du Seuil, Paris, 1977, page 90.
Catalogue for the Exhibition "Joan Miró". Exhibition Room of the Caixa d'Estalvis i Mont de Pietat de Barcelona, Manresa (Barcelona), 1977, No. 54.
Catalogue for the Exhibition "Joan Miró. Obra Gráfica". Halls of the Dirección General del Patrimonio Artístico, Archivos y Museos, Madrid, 1978, page 85, No. 238.
Catalogue for the Exhibition "Joan Miró. Obra gràfica". Exhibition Room of the Caixa d'Estalvis Laietana, Mataró (Barcelona), 1978, No. 16.

UN CAMÍ COMPARTIT
(MIRÓ - MAEGHT)
galeria maeght, barcelona. 5 desembre 1975 – 31 gener 1976

88. "AVUI". 1976.

Poster produced for the presentation of the Catalan newspaper "Avui" (April 1976).

Publication:
5,000 copies on standard paper.
Size: 65.5 × 52 cm.

100 copies *avant la lettre* on Arches paper, numbered and signed.
Printing process: colour lithographic press.
Size: 81 × 61.5 cm.

Publisher: Avui, Barcelona.
Printer: Litografías Artísticas Damià Caus, Barcelona.

BIBLIOGRAPHY:

JOHANSSON, Kjell A.: *Miró en Escania*. "Dagens Nyheter", Stockholm, 30 June 1976.

Catalogue for the Exhibition "Joan Miró. Obra Gráfica". Halls of the Dirección General del Patrimonio Artístico, Archivos y Museos, Madrid, 1978, page 85, No. 235.

Catalogue for the Exhibition "Joan Miró. Obra gràfica". Exhibition Room of the Caixa d'Estalvis Laietana, Mataró (Barcelona), 1978, No. 32.

"Mundo Diario", Barcelona, 16 November 1978.

89. "QUIRIQUIBÚ". 1976.

Poster produced by Miró for the presentation of the play *Quiriquibú* by Joan Brossa at the Aliança del Poble Nou Theatre, Barcelona.

Publication:
2,000 copies on standard paper.
Size: 75 × 56 cm.

99 copies *avant la lettre* on Guarro paper, numbered and signed.
Printing process: colour lithographic press.
Size: 75 × 56 cm.

Publisher: Ed. Polígrafa, S.A., Barcelona.
Printer: La Polígrafa, S.A., Barcelona.

BIBLIOGRAPHY:

Catalogue for the Exhibition "Joan Miró. Obra gràfica". Exhibition Room of the Caixa d'Estalvis Laietana, Mataró (Barcelona), 1978, No. 36.

QUIRI
QUIBU

JOAN BROSSA

90. FORMAL INAUGURATION OF THE FUNDACIÓ JOAN MIRÓ. 1976.

Poster produced for the inauguration of the Fundació Joan Miró, Centre d'Estudis d'Art Contemporani, in Barcelona (18, 19 and 20 June 1976).

This poster was later used for the presentation in Catalonia of the play based on Joanot Martorell's novel *Tirant lo Blanc* (August 1976).

Publication:
2,000 copies on standard paper.
Size: 70 × 50 cm.

90 copies *avant la lettre* on Guarro paper, numbered and signed.
Printing process: colour lithographic press.
Size: 70 × 50 cm.

Publisher: Fundació Joan Miró, Barcelona.
Printer: La Polígrafa, S.A., Barcelona.

BIBLIOGRAPHY:

Catalogue for the Exhibition "Joan Miró. Obra Gráfica". Halls of the Dirección General del Patrimonio Artístico, Archivos y Museos, Madrid, 1978, page 85, No. 240.
"Avui", Barcelona, 20 April 1978, page 14.

FUNDACIÓ JOAN MIRÓ
Centre d'Estudis d'Art Contemporani

Parc de Montjuïc   **BARCELONA**
Inauguració: 18, 19 i 20 de juny de 1976

Hores de visita: Cada dia de les onze del matí a les vuit del vespre (exceptuant els dilluns)

91. "JOAN MIRÓ: EL PI DE FORMENTOR" EXHIBITION. 1976.

Poster for the presentation at the Galeria 4 Gats, Palma de Mallorca, of two books illustrated by Miró, *El Pi de Formentor* by Miquel Costa i Llobera and *Cinc poemes de Salvador Espriu,* published by the Sala Gaspar, Barcelona (June-July 1976).

Publication:
2,000 copies on standard paper.
Size: 71 × 52.5 cm.

100 copies *avant la lettre* on Guarro paper, numbered and signed.
Printing process: colour lithographic press.
Size: 81.5 × 58 cm.

Publisher: Galeria 4 Gats, Palma de Mallorca.
Printer: Litografías Artísticas Damià Caus, Barcelona.

Juny – Juliol 1976 – Galeria 4 Gats·c/. Sant Sebastiá, 7 – Palma

92. "CENTENARI DEL CENTRE EXCURSIONISTA DE CATALUNYA". 1976.

Poster produced for the centenary of the Centre Excursionista de Catalunya, Barcelona.

Publication:
10,000 copies on standard paper.
Size: 69 × 52 cm.

100 copies *avant la lettre* on Arches paper, numbered and signed.
Printing process: colour lithographic press.
Size: 82 × 63 cm.

Publisher: Centre Excursionista de Catalunya, Barcelona.
Printer: Litografías Artísticas Damià Caus, Barcelona.

BIBLIOGRAPHY:

"Tele-Exprés", Barcelona, 29 April 1975.
"La Vanguardia Española", Barcelona, 12 February 1976.
Centenari Centre Excursionista de Catalunya: Homenatge dels artistes catalans. Ed. Martí March, Barcelona, 1976, page 233.
"Avui", Barcelona, 20 April 1978, page 14.
Catalogue for the Exhibition "Joan Miró, Obra Gráfica". Halls of the Dirección General del Patrimonio Artístico, Archivos y Museos, Madrid, 1978, page 85, No. 236.
Catalogue for the Exhibition "Joan Miró. Obra gràfica". Exhibition Room of the Caixa d'Estalvis Laietana, Mataró (Barcelona), 1978, No. 35.

CENTENARI
DEL CENTRE EXCURSIONISTA
DE CATALUNYA

1876
1976

93. "AMNESTY INTERNATIONAL". 1976.

Poster produced by Miró for Amnesty International based in New York.

This poster, scaled down to 74.5×48 cm., was later used for the exhibition "Artistas por la Amnistía" held at the Fundació Joan Miró, Barcelona (10 December 1976 to 9 January 1977). It was published with Spanish and Catalan texts by Amnesty International, Barcelona and printed by La Polígrafa, S.A., Barcelona.

Publication:
Indefinite number of copies on standard paper.
Size: 90×61 cm.

100 copies *avant la lettre* on special paper, numbered and signed.
Printing process: colour lithographic press.
Size: 90×61 cm.

Publisher: Amnesty International, New York.
Printer: Arte Adrien Maeght, Paris.

BIBLIOGRAPHY:

JOHANSSON, Kjell A.: *Miró en Escania*. "Dagens Nyheter", Stockholm, 30 June 1976.
Catalogue for the Exhibition "Joan Miró. Obra Gráfica". Halls of the Dirección General del Patrimonio Artístico, Archivos y Museos, Madrid, 1978, page 85, No. 237.
"Avui", Barcelona, 20 April 1978, page 14.
"El País", Madrid, 28 May 1978.
Catalogue for the Exhibition "Joan Miró. Obra gràfica". Exhibition Room of the Caixa d'Estalvis Laietana, Mataró (Barcelona), 1978, No. 34.

94. "MIRÓ-REUS" EXHIBITION. 1977.

Poster for the exhibition of Miró's graphic work at the Centre de Lectura, Reus, Tarragona (27 June to 30 July 1977).

Publication:
500 copies on standard paper.
Size: 59 × 40.5 cm.

50 copies *avant la lettre* on Arches paper, numbered and signed.
Printing process: colour lithographic press.
Size: 75 × 55 cm.

Publisher: Centre de Lectura, Reus.
Printer (poster): A. Rabassa, Reus.
Printer *(avant la lettre):* Arte Adrien Maeght, Paris.

Exposició obra gràfica

JOAN MIRÓ

Homenatge als poetes catalans

Del 27 de Juny al 30 Juliol 1977 - De 5 a 9 tarda.

CENTRE DE LECTURA - Major, 15 - R E U S

95. "MIRÓ-CÉRET" EXHIBITION. 1977.

Poster for the exhibition of Miró's painting, sculpture and graphic work at the Musée d'Art Moderne, Céret (July, August and September 1977).

Publication:
2,000 copies on standard paper.
Size: 76 × 54.5 cm.

50 copies *avant la lettre* on Arches paper, numbered and signed.
Printing process: colour lithographic press.
Size: 75.5 × 55.5 cm.

Publisher: Musée d'Art Moderne, Céret.
Printer: Arte Adrien Maeght, Paris.

MUSÉE D'ART MODERNE
juillet-août-septembre 1977

96. "CONGRÉS DE CULTURA CATALANA". 1977.

Poster produced by Miró for the Congrés de Cultura Catalana in 1977.

Publication:
7,000 copies on standard paper.
Size: 75.5 × 56.5 cm.

100 copies *avant la lettre* on Arches paper, numbered and signed.
Printing process: colour lithographic press.
Size: 84 × 63 cm.

Publisher: Congrés de Cultura Catalana, Barcelona.
Printer: Litografías Artísticas Damià Caus, Barcelona.

BIBLIOGRAPHY:

"Mundo Diario", Barcelona, 24 March 1977.
Catalogue for the Exhibition "Joan Miró". Exhibition Room of the Caixa d'Estalvis i Mont de Pietat de Barcelona, Manresa (Barcelona), 1977, No. 61.
"Avui", Barcelona, 20 April 1978, page 14.
Catalogue for the Exhibition "Joan Miró. Obra gràfica". Exhibition Room of the Caixa d'Estalvis Laietana, Mataró (Barcelona), 1978, No. 38.

Congrés de Cultura Catalana 1977

97. "VOLEM L'ESTATUT". 1977.

Poster for the campaign *Volem l'Estatut* in Catalonia to obtain the Statute of Autonomy.

Colour lithograph: 75×54 cm.

BIBLIOGRAPHY:

RAILLARD, Georges: *Conversaciones con Miró*. Granica Editor, Barcelona, 1978, pages 232-233.

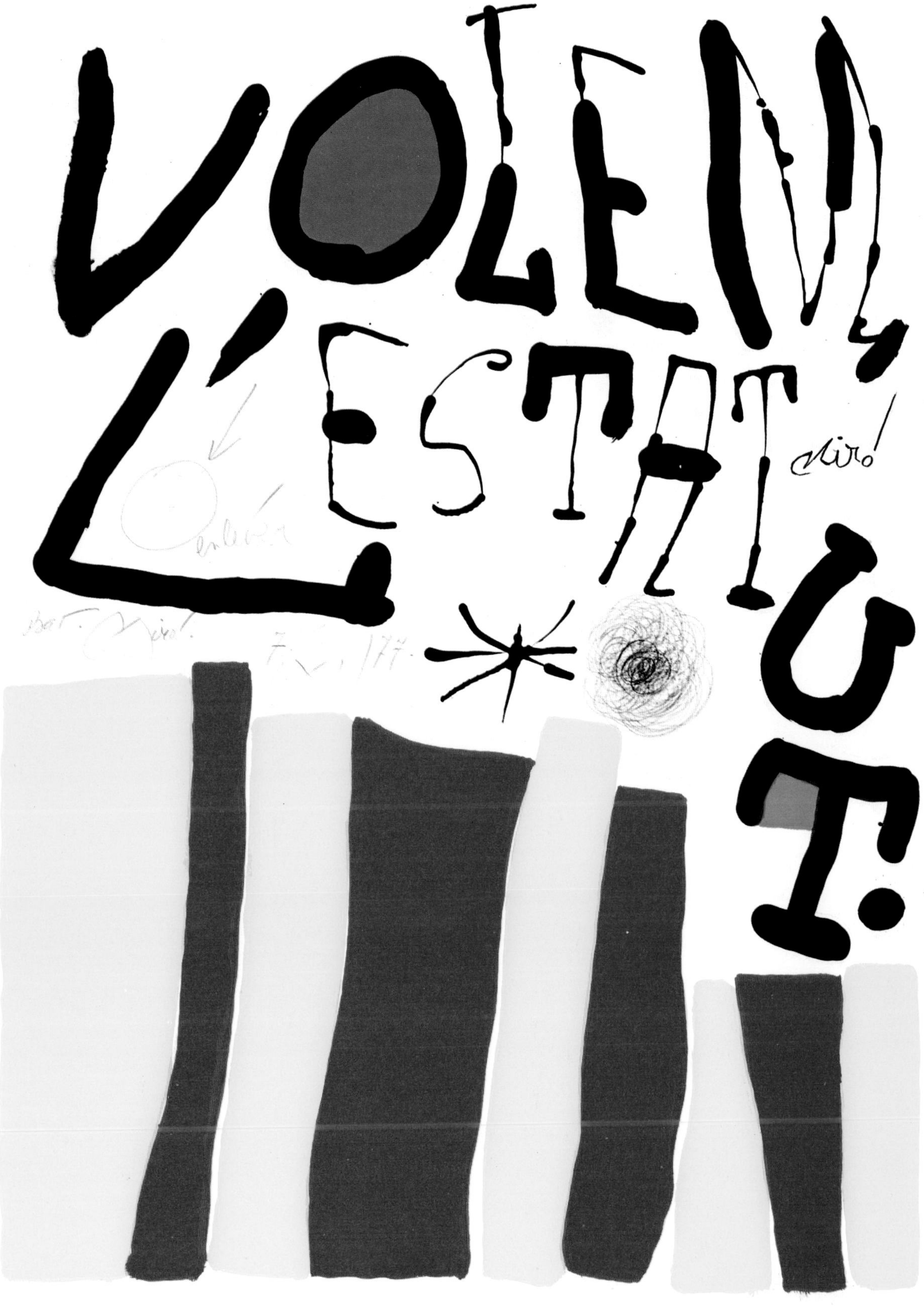
VOLEM L'ESTATUT.
Miró

98. "MIRÓ A PICASSO" EXHIBITION. 1978.

Poster by Miró based on his drawing in India ink and wax colours *Personaje* (1975), for the exhibition "Miró a Picasso" at the Sala Gaspar, Barcelona (April-May 1978).

Publication:
500 copies on standard paper.
Size: 66 × 46.5 cm.

Publisher: Sala Gaspar, Barcelona.
Printer: Gráficas Universidad, Barcelona.

ABRIL-MAIG 1978   BARCELONA

99. "MIRÓ-PINTURA" EXHIBITION. 1978.

Poster produced for the retrospective exhibition of Miró's painting at the Museo Español de Arte Contemporáneo, Madrid (4 May to 23 July 1978).

This poster was later used for the exhibition "XVIII Concurso Internacional de Dibujo Joan Miró en Barcelona", at the Galerie Orizont, Bucharest (October-November 1979).

Publication:
5,000 copies on standard paper.
Size: 70 × 51 cm.

99 copies *avant la lettre* on Guarro paper, numbered and signed.
Printing process: colour lithographic press.
Size: 70 × 51 cm.

Publisher: Ministerio de Cultura, Madrid.
Printer: La Polígrafa, S.A., Barcelona.

BIBLIOGRAPHY:

"La Actualidad Española", Madrid, No. 1351, 14 May 1978, page 50.

DIRECCIÓN GENERAL DEL PATRIMONIO ARTÍSTICO, ARCHIVOS Y MUSEOS

con la colaboración de la
FUNDACIÓN MIRÓ

MINISTERIO DE CULTURA

MUSEO ESPAÑOL
DE ARTE CONTEMPORÁNEO
Av. Juan de Herrera · s/n
Ciudad Universitaria · Madrid

4 mayo - 23 julio 1978

PINTURA

100. "MIRÓ-OBRA GRÁFICA" EXHIBITION. 1978.

Poster produced for the retrospective exhibition of graphic work, illustrated books and posters by Miró in the Halls of the Dirección General del Patrimonio Artístico, Archivos y Museos in Madrid (4 May to 23 July 1978).

Publication:
5,000 copies on standard paper.
Size: 70 × 51 cm.

99 copies *avant la lettre* on Guarro paper, numbered and signed.
Printing process: colour lithographic press.
Size: 70 × 51 cm.

Publisher: Ministerio de Cultura, Madrid.
Printer: La Polígrafa, S.A., Barcelona.

BIBLIOGRAPHY:

"La Actualidad Española", Madrid, No. 1351, 15 May 1978, page 50.

DIRECCIÓN GENERAL
DEL PATRIMONIO ARTÍSTICO,
ARCHIVOS Y MUSEOS
con la colaboración de la
FUNDACIÓN
MIRÓ

MINISTERIO DE
CULTURA

OBRA GRÁFICA

Salas de la Dirección General
del Patrimonio Artístico,
Archivos y Museos

Calvo Sotelo, 20 · Madrid

4 mayo - 23 julio 1978

101. JOAN MIRÓ EXHIBITION AT THE GALERIA THEO. 1978.

Poster produced for the exhibition of 36 paintings by Miró at the Galería Theo, Madrid, in honour of the artist's 85th birthday (5 May-June 1978).

Publication:
413 copies on standard paper.
Size: 62.5 × 43.5 cm.

20 copies *avant la lettre* on Guarro paper, signed and dated.
Printing process: colour offset.
Size: 62.5 × 43.5 cm.

Publisher: Galeria Theo, Madrid.
Printer: Luis Pérez, Madrid.

BIBLIOGRAPHY:

"Guadalimar", Madrid, Year 4, No. 32, May 1978, back cover.

Joan Miró

Pinturas de 1916-1974

Mayo/Junio 1978

galería theo   Marqués de la Ensenada, 2 - Madrid-4

102. GALERIA MAEGHT-BARCELONA EXHIBITION. 1978.

Poster for the exhibition of 117 works by Miró —drawings, gouaches and monotypes— at the Galeria Maeght, Barcelona (10 May to 30 June 1978).

This poster was later used for the presentation of the same exhibition at the Sala Pelaires, Palma de Mallorca (15 November-December 1978) and at the Galería de Exposiciones del Banco de Granada (December 1978-January 1979).

Publication:
7,000 copies on standard paper.
Size: 73 × 48.5 cm.

75 copies *avant la lettre* on Arches paper, numbered and signed.
Printing process: colour lithographic press.
Size: 90 × 62.5 cm.

Publisher: Galeria Maeght, Barcelona.
Printer: Litografías Artísticas Damià Caus, Barcelona.

BIBLIOGRAPHY:

Catalogue for the Exhibition "Joan Miró. Obra gràfica". Exhibition Room of the Caixa d'Estalvis Laietana, Mataró (Barcelona), 1978, Nos. 25 and 39.

103. "MORI EL MERMA". 1978.

Poster produced for the presentation of the play *Mori el Merma* by the Claca Theatre Company, with décor, masks and costumes by Miró, at the Gran Teatro del Liceo in Barcelona (7-12 June 1978).

Publication:
2,000 copies on standard paper.
Size: 94 × 65 cm.

Publisher: Caixa de Pensions per a la Vellesa i d'Estalvis, Barcelona.
Printer: La Polígrafa, S.A., Barcelona.

BIBLIOGRAPHY:

"Última hora", Palma de Mallorca, September 1978. Special issue devoted to Joan Miró.
Mori el Merma. Obra Cultural de la Caixa de Pensions per a la Vellesa i d'Estalvis, Barcelona, 1978. Front cover.

MORI EL MERMA
COMPANYIA DE TEATRE CLACA

GRAN TEATRE DEL LICEU DE BARCELONA
DEL 7 AL 12 DE JUNY 1978, A DOS QUARTS D'ONZE DE LA NIT
PREUS: 300 PESSETES; 100 PESSETES

VENDA ANTICIPADA DE LOCALITATS AL MATEIX LICEU

PATROCINAT PER
L'OBRA CULTURAL
DE LA CAIXA DE PENSIONS PER A LA VELLESA I D'ESTALVIS

CAIXA DE PENSIONS
"la Caixa"
de Catalunya i Balears

104. "OBRA CULTURAL BALEAR". 1978.

Poster produced by Miró in support of the association Obra Cultural Balear, Palma de Mallorca.

Publication:
Indefinite number of copies on standard paper.
Size: 74 × 58 cm.

75 copies *avant la lettre* on Arches paper, numbered and signed.
Printing process: colour lithographic press.
Size: 59 × 58.5 cm.

Publisher: Obra Cultural Balear, Palma de Mallorca.
Printer: Litografías Artísticas Damià Caus, Barcelona.

BIBLIOGRAPHY:

"Serra d'Or", Abadía de Montserrat (Barcelona), No. 236, 10 May 1979, front cover.

OBRA CULTURAL BALEAR

cada poble llaura el seu futur

105. "SA LLOTJA" EXHIBITION. 1978.

Poster for Miró's retrospective exhibition at the Stock Exchange (Sa Llotja) building, Palma de Mallorca (4 September to October 1978).

Publication:
8,000 copies on standard paper.
Size: 92 × 64 cm.

100 copies *avant la lettre* on Arches paper, numbered and signed.
Printing process: colour lithographic press.
Size: 92 × 64 cm.

Publisher: Palma de Mallorca Town Council.
Printer: Litografías Artísticas Damià Caus, Barcelona.

BIBLIOGRAPHY:

"Última Hora", Palma de Mallorca, September 1978. Special issue devoted to Joan Miró.

"Destino", Barcelona, 28 October 1978.

Catalogue for the Exhibition "Joan Miró. Obra gràfica". Exhibition Rooms of the Caixa d'Estalvis Laietana, Mataró (Barcelona), 1978, No. 40.

106. "CENTRE D'ÉTUDES CATALANES" EXHIBITION. 1978.

Poster for the exhibition of Miró's graphic work at the Centre d'Études Catalanes, Paris (3 October to 10 November 1978).

Publication:
1,500 copies on standard paper.
Size: 65 × 46.5 cm.

75 copies *avant la lettre* on Arches paper, numbered and signed.
Printing process: colour lithographic press.
Size: 75 × 55 cm.

Publisher: Centre d'Études Catalanes, Paris.
Publisher: Arte Adrien Maeght, Paris.

eaux-fortes
gravures pour des poèmes de Salvador Espriu

3 octobre - 10 novembre 1978

Centre d'études catalanes

Université de Paris-Sorbonne, 9 rue Sainte-Croix-de-la-Bretonnerie 75004 Paris, ouvert de 10 heures à 19 heures

Imp. Arte

107. "100 SCULPTURES" EXHIBITION. 1978.

Poster for Miró's exhibition "100 Sculptures" (1962-1978), at the Musée d'Art Moderne de la Ville de Paris (19 October to 17 December 1978).

Publication:
5,000 copies on standard paper.
Size: 68 × 46.5 cm.

75 copies *avant la lettre* on Arches paper, numbered and signed.
Printing process: colour lithographic press.
Size: 72 × 52 cm.

Publisher: Musée d'Art Moderne de la Ville de Paris.
Printer: Arte Adrien Maeght, Paris.

This lithograph — with the inversion of the lithographic stone and the modification of some of the colours — was used for the poster advertising the exhibition of 70 works by Miró at the Seibu Museum of Art, Tokyo (2 January to 25 February 1977).

Publication:
2,000 copies on standard paper.
Size: 71 × 49.5 cm.

75 copies *avant la lettre* on Arches paper, numbered and signed.
Printing process: colour lithographic press.
Size: 71 × 49.5 cm.

Publisher: The Seibu Museum of Art, Tokyo.
Printer: Arte Adrien Maeght, Paris.

BIBLIOGRAPHY:

Catalogue for the Exhibition "Joan Miró". The Seibu Museum of Art, Tokyo, 1979.

100 sculptures
1962 - 1978

19 octobre - 17 décembre 1978

Musée d'art moderne de la Ville de Paris

Avenue du Président-Wilson. Ouvert tous les jours de 10 h à 17 h 40 sauf le lundi et le mardi

ARTE · PARIS

108. GALERIE MAEGHT EXHIBITION. 1978.

Poster produced for the exhibition of 51 printings by Miró at the Galerie Maeght, Paris (22 November 1978 to 19 January 1979).

Publication:
10,000 copies on standard paper.
Size: 76.5 × 55.5 cm.
60 copies on standard paper.
Size: 160 × 120 cm.

75 copies *avant la lettre* on Arches paper, numbered and signed.
Printing process: colour lithographic press.
Size: 78 × 57 cm.

Publisher: Galerie Maeght, Paris.
Printer: Arte Adrien Maeght, Paris.

BIBLIOGRAPHY:

Catalogue "Affiches - Posters 1979". Maeght Éd., Paris, 1979, No. 169.

22 NOVEMBRE 1978 - 19 JANVIER 1979

GALERIE MAEGHT

13 RUE DE TÉHÉRAN ET 26 RUE TREILHARD PARIS 8

109. JOSEP-LLUÍS SERT EXHIBITION. 1978.

Poster produced by Joan Miró for the exhibition of the architect Josep-Lluís Sert at the Carpenter Center for the Visual Arts of Harvard University, Cambridge, Massachusetts (2 December to 1 February 1979).

Publication:
1,000 copies on standard paper.
Size: 66 × 45 cm.

25 copies *avant la lettre* on Arches paper, numbered and signed.
Printing process: colour lithographic press.
Size: 66 × 45 cm.

Publisher: Carpenter Center for the Visual Arts, Cambridge, Mass.
Printer: Arte Adrien Maeght, Paris.

Carpenter Center for the Visual Arts
Harvard University

December 2nd 1978 - February 1st 1979

Imp. Arte

110. "LA CAIXA - 75 ANYS". 1979.

Poster produced by Miró to celebrate the 75th Anniversary of the Caixa de Pensions per a la Vellesa i d'Estalvis de Catalunya i Balears.

Publication:
15,000 copies on standard paper.
Size: 90 × 65 cm.

100 copies *avant la lettre* on Arches paper, numbered and signed.
Printing process: colour lithographic press.
Size: 90 × 63 cm.

Publisher: Caixa de Pensions per a la Vellesa i d'Estalvis de Catalunya i Balears, Barcelona.
  Printer: Litografías Artísticas Damià Caus, Barcelona.

BIBLIOGRAPHY:

Quaderns de l'obra social. Caixa de Pensions per a la Vellesa i d'Estalvis, Barcelona, No. 1, May 1979, front cover.

111. MARIA CANALS SINGING COMPETITION. 1979.

Poster produced by Miró for the presentation of the XXVth International Maria Canals Singing Competition (18 March to 2 April 1979).

The same base as for the 1978 poster *Miró a Picasso* (No. 98), modified by Miró himself, has been used for this poster.

Publication:
1,200 copies on standard paper.
Size: 70 × 50 cm.

Publisher: Concurso Maria Canals, Barcelona.
Printer: Gráficas Universidad, Barcelona.

BIBLIOGRAPHY

"La Vanguardia Española", Barcelona, 18 March 1979.

XXV Aniversari   18 de març - 2 d'abril 1979
Casal del Metge - Palau de la Música Catalana
Barcelona

112. "FONDATION MAEGHT" EXHIBITION. 1979.

Poster produced for the exhibition of 378 works by Miró — painting, sculpture, drawings, ceramics and graphic work — at the Maeght Foundation, Saint-Paul-de-Vence (7 July to 30 September 1979).

Publication:
7,700 copies on standard paper.
Size: 86 × 50 cm.

75 copies *avant la lettre* on Arches paper, numbered and signed.
Printing process: colour lithographic press.
Size: 90 × 61 cm.

Publisher: Fondation Maeght, Saint-Paul-de-Vence.
Printer: Les Artisans Lithographes, Paris.

miró

7 juillet - 30 septembre 1979

fondation maeght

06570 saint-paul

113. "HOMENATGE A GAUDÍ" EXHIBITION. 1979.

Poster produced for the exhibition "Homenatge a Gaudí", made up of 100 engravings and 4 sculptures by Miró, at the Galería Maeght, Barcelona (29 May to July 1979).

Publication:
2,000 copies on standard paper.
Size: 75.5 × 52.5 cm.

75 copies *avant la lettre* on Arches paper, numbered and signed.
Printing process: colour lithographic press.
Size: 89.5 × 62 cm.

Publisher: Galeria Maeght, Barcelona.
Printer: Litografías Artísticas Damià Caus, Barcelona.

114. "MIL LLIBRES EN CATALÀ". 1979.

Poster produced by Miró for Edicions 62, Barcelona, to celebrate the publication of their 1,000th book in Catalan.

This drawing was also used for the cover of the book *Edicions 62. 1.000 llibres en català. 1962-1979.*

Publication:
3,000 copies on standard paper.
Size: 62.5 × 31.5 cm.

Publisher: Edicions 62, Barcelona.
Printer: Selegram, Barcelona.

BIBLIOGRAPHY:

"Tele-Exprés", Barcelona, 27 December 1979, page 17.

mil llibres en català

(1962-1979)

edicions 62

SELEGRAM Pallars 94-96 Barna-18 D.L.B 40.716/79

115. "ŒUVRES SUR PAPIER, PEINTURES, GRAPHIQUES" EXHIBITION. 1980.

Poster produced for the exhibition of paintings, drawings, paintings on paper and graphic work by Miró, at the Isetan Museum, Tokyo (26 January-March 1980).

Publication:
1,500 copies on standard paper.
Size: 87 × 59 cm.

35 copies *avant la lettre* on Arches paper, numbered and signed.
Printing process: colour lithographic press.
Size: 76 × 57 cm.

Publisher: Isetan Museum, Tokyo.
Printer: Litografías Artísticas Damià Caus, Barcelona.

OEUVRES SUR PAPIER, PEINTURES, GRAPHIQUES

 '80

MUSÉE ISETAN

116. "SERT - MIRÓ - FOIX - LLORENS ARTIGAS"
EXHIBITION. 1980.

Poster produced by Miró, with a collage of photographs by the photographer
Català-Roca, for the exhibition "Sert - Miró - Foix - Llorens Artigas" at the
Galeria Artema, Barcelona (15 April to 15 May 1980).

Publication:
1,000 copies on standard paper.
Size: 86.5 × 55.5 cm.

Publisher: Artema, Barcelona.
Printer: Gráficas Universidad, Barcelona.

ARTEMA

rbla. catalunya 42 barcelona 7 del 15 de abril al 15 de maig de 1980

117. "MUSEO DE ARTE MODERNO DE MÉXICO"
EXHIBITION. 1980.

Poster produced for the exhibition at the Museo de Arte Moderno de México (May to August 1980).

Publication:
1,600 copies on standard paper.
Size: 76 × 56 cm.

100 copies *avant la lettre* on Arches paper, numbered and signed.
Printing process: colour lithographic press.
Size: 76 × 56 cm.

Publishers: Museo de Arte Moderno, Mexico.
Printer: Litografías Artísticas Damià Caus, Barcelona.

MAYO / AGOSTO

MUSEO DE ARTE MODERNO
BOSQUE DE CHAPULTEPEC
INBA INSTITUTO NACIONAL DE BELLAS ARTES/FONDO NACIONAL PARA ACTIVIDADES SOCIALES
MEXICO, D.F., 1980

Litografias Artisticas Dep. Legal B-43261

118. "HOMENATGE A J. TORRES CLAVÉ" EXHIBITION. 1980.

Poster produced by Miró for the exhibition in homage to the architect Josep Torres Clavé (1906-1938), organized by the Colegio de Arquitectos de Cataluña and the architectural review *2C. Construcció de la ciutat,* and held at the premises of the Colegio in Barcelona (15 May to 11 June 1980).

Publication:
1,000 copies on standard paper.
1,500 copies on standard paper, without the printed text.
Size: 66×50.5 cm.

Publisher: Colegio de Arquitectos de Cataluña, Barcelona.
Printer: Litografías Artísticas Damià Caus, Barcelona.

HOMENATGE A J TORRES CLAVE

col·legi d'arquitectes de catalunya
2c construccio de la ciutat.
barcelona plaça nova 5. maig · 1980

119. "60 VOLTA CICLISTA A CATALUNYA". 1980.

Poster done by Miró for the 60th "Volta Ciclista a Catalunya" (Bicycle race), from 3 to 10 September 1980.

Printing:
8,000 copies on standard paper.
Format: 56 × 37,8 cm.

75 copies *avant la lettre* on Arches paper, numbered and signed.
Printing process: colour lithographic press.
Format: 76 × 52 cm.

Publisher: Caixa de Pensions per a la Vellesa i d'Estalvis, Barcelona.
Printer (for the poster): Gráficas Reclam, Barcelona.
Printer *avant la lettre:* Litografías Artísticas Damià Caus, Barcelona.

BIBLIOGRAPHY:

"El Noticiero Universal", Barcelona, 20 June 1980.
"Avui", Barcelona, 21 June 1980.

Del 3 al 10 de Setembre de 1980

ORGANITZACIÓ:
SECCIÓ DE CICLISME
DE LA UNIÓ ESPORTIVA
DE SANTS

GRAN PREMI
CAIXA DE PENSIONS
"la Caixa"

SOTA EL PATROCINI
DE LA GENERALITAT

Amb la col·laboració de:
SPORT

Graf.RECLAM 7-80 Dep.Legal B.25638-1980

INDEX
OF ILLUSTRATIONS

40. PRESENTATION OF THREE BOOKS ON MIRÓ IN JAPAN. 1970. Ed. Polígrafa, S.A., Barcelona.

41. "SCULPTURES" EXHIBITION. 1970. Galerie Maeght, Paris.

42. "SCULPTURES" EXHIBITION 1970. Galerie Maeght, Paris.

43. "MIRÓ, SALA GASPAR-BARCELONA" EXHIBITION. 1970. Sala Gaspar, Barcelona.

44. "MIRÓ SALA PELAIRES" EXHIBITION. 1970. Sala Pelaires, Palma de Mallorca.

45. "LLORENS ARTIGAS-JOANET ARTIGAS" EXHIBITION. 1971. Sala Pelaires, Palma de Mallorca.

46. "1.ª MUESTRA INTERNACIONAL DE ARTE. HOMENAJE A JOAN MIRÓ" EXHIBITION. 1971. Granollers Town Council (Barcelona).

47. "AGORA 1" EXHIBITION. 1971. Musée d'Art Moderne, Strasbourg.

48. "HOMENATGE A JOAN PRATS" EXHIBITION. 1971. Ed. Polígrafa, S.A., Barcelona.

49. "MIRÓ SCULPTURES" EXHIBITION. 1971. Walker Art Center, Minneapolis.

50. "II CONGRESO JURÍDICO CATALÁN". 1971. Colegio de Abogados de Barcelona.

51. "PEINTURES SUR PAPIER-DESSINS" EXHIBITION. 1971. Galerie Maeght, Paris.

52. "PEINTURES SUR PAPIER-DESSINS" EXHIBITION. 1971. Galerie Maeght, Paris.

53. "LE LÉZARD AUX PLUMES D'OR". 1971. Galerie Berggruen, Paris.

54. "QÜESTIONS D'ART". 1971. Qüestions d'Art, Barcelona.

55. "HOMENAJE A JOSEP-LLUÍS SERT" EXHIBITION. 1972. Colegio de Arquitectos de Canarias, Santa Cruz de Tenerife.

56. "HOMENATGE A JOAN PRATS" EXHIBITION. 1972. Galerie Berggruen, Paris.

57. "MIRÓ BRONZES" EXHIBITION. 1972. Arts Council, London.

58. "SOBRETEIXIMS I ESCULTURES" EXHIBITION. 1972. Sala Gaspar, Barcelona.

59. "PEINTURES, GOUACHES, DESSINS" EXHIBITION. 1972. Galerie Maeght, Zürich.

60. "DAS PLASTISCHE WERK" EXHIBITION. 1972. Kunsthaus, Zürich.

61. "HOMENATGE A JOSEP-LLUÍS SERT I JOSEP LLORENS ARTIGAS" EXHIBITION. 1972. Colegio de Arquitectos de Cataluña y Baleares, Barcelona.

62. "DAS GRAPHISCHE WERK" EXHIBITION. 1973. Kunstverein, Hamburg.

63. "SÈRIE MALLORCA" EXHIBITION. 1973. Sala Pelaires, Palma de Mallorca.

64. "SOBRETEIXIMS" EXHIBITION. 1973. Galerie Maeght, Paris.

65. "SCULPTURES ET CÉRAMIQUES" EXHIBITION. 1973. Fondation Maeght, Saint-Paul-de-Vence.

66. "KRISTIANSTADS MUSEUM" EXHIBITION. 1973. Société des Admirateurs de Joan Miró.

67. "SCULPTURES EN MONTAGNE" EXHIBITION. 1973. Sculptures en Montagne, Passy.

68. "ŒUVRE GRAVÉ ORIGINAL" EXHIBITION. 1973. Musée de l'Athénée, Geneva.

69. "LIVRES ILLUSTRÉS ET LITHOGRAPHIES" EXHIBITION. 1973. Galerie Gérald Cramer, Geneva.

70. "HOMAGE TO MIRÓ" EXHIBITION. 1973. Museum of Modern Art, New York.

71. "UNIVERSITÉ DE GENÈVE". 1973. Université de Genève, Geneva.

72. "MALLORCA". 1973. Consejo del Fomento de Turismo, Palma de Mallorca.

73. "YOUNG ARTISTS '73" EXHIBITION. 1973. International Play Group, New York.

74. "UMBRACLE". 1973. Pere Portabella, Barcelona.

75. "PER UN TEATRE A CATALUNYA". 1973. Sala Gaspar, Barcelona.

76. "MIRÓ-GRAND PALAIS" EXHIBITION. 1974. Réunion des Musées Nationaux, Paris.

77. "MIRÓ-GRAND PALAIS" EXHIBITION. 1974. Réunion des Musées Nationaux, Paris.

78. "MIRÓ, L'ŒUVRE GRAPHIQUE" EXHIBITION. 1974. Musée d'Art Moderne de la Ville de Paris.

79. OPENING OF THE GALERIA MAEGHT-BARCELONA EXHIBITION. 1974. Galeria Maeght, Barcelona.

80. "OBRA GRÁFICA-FUNDAÇÀO GULBENKIAN" EXHIBITION. 1974. Gulbenkian Foundation, Lisbon.

81. "ÒMNIUM CULTURAL". 1974. Omnium Cultural, Barcelona.

82. "FUTBOL CLUB BARCELONA". 1974. Futbol Club Barcelona, Barcelona.

83. "UNESCO-DROITS DE L'HOMME". 1974. Unesco, Paris.

84. "LOUISIANA" EXHIBITION. 1974. Louisiana Modern Art Museum, Humleback.

85. OPENING OF THE FUNDACIÓ JOAN MIRÓ. 1975. Fundació Joan Miró, Barcelona.

86. "LUCIFER". 1975. Galerie Maeght, Paris.

87. "UN CAMÍ COMPARTIT (MIRÓ-MAEGHT)" EXHIBITION. 1975. Galeria Maeght, Barcelona.

88. "AVUI". 1976. Avui, Barcelona.

89. "QUIRIQUIBÚ". 1976. Ed. Polígrafa, S.A., Barcelona.

90. FORMAL INAUGURATION OF THE FUNDACIÓ JOAN MIRÓ. 1976. Fundació Joan Miró, Barcelona.

91. "JOAN MIRÓ: EL PI DE FORMENTOR" EXHIBITION. 1976. Galeria 4 Gats, Palma de Mallorca.

92. "CENTENARI DEL CENTRE EXCURSIONISTA DE CATALUNYA". 1976. Centre Excursionista de Catalunya, Barcelona.

93. "AMNESTY INTERNATIONAL". 1976. Amnesty International, New York.

94. "MIRÓ-REUS" EXHIBITION. 1977. Centre de Lectura, Reus.

95. "MIRÓ-CÉRET" EXHIBITION. 1977. Musée d'Art Moderne, Céret

96. "CONGRÉS DE CULTURA CATALANA". 1977. Congrés de Cultura Catalana, Barcelona.

97. "VOLEM L'ESTATUT". 1977.

98. "MIRÓ A PICASSO" EXHIBITION. 1978. Sala Gaspar, Barcelona.

99. "MIRÓ-PINTURA" EXHIBITION. 1978. Ministerio de Cultura, Madrid.

100. "MIRÓ-OBRA GRÁFICA" EXHIBITION. 1978. Ministerio de Cultura, Madrid.

101. "JOAN MIRÓ" EXHIBITION AT THE GALERIA THEO. 1978. Galería Theo, Madrid.

102. GALERIA MAEGHT-BARCELONA EXHIBITION. 1978. Galeria Maeght, Barcelona.

103. "MORI EL MERMA". 1978. Caixa de Pensions per a la Vellesa i d'Estalvis, Barcelona.

104. "OBRA CULTURAL BALEAR". 1978. Obra Cultural Balear, Palma de Mallorca.

105. "SA LLOTJA" EXHIBITION. 1978. Palma de Mallorca Town Council.

106. "CENTRE D'ÉTUDES CATALANES" EXHIBITION. 1978. Centre d'Études Catalanes, Paris.

107. "100 SCULPTURES" EXHIBITION. 1978. Musée d'Art Moderne de la Ville de Paris.

108. GALERIE MAEGHT EXHIBITION. 1978. Galerie Maeght, Paris.

109. JOSEP-LLUIS SERT EXHIBITION. 1978. Carpenter Center for the Visual Arts, Cambridge, Mass.

110. "LA CAIXA - 75 ANYS". 1979. Caixa de Pensions per a la Vellesa i d'Estalvis de Catalunya i Balears, Barcelona.

111. MARIA CANALS SINGING COMPETITION. 1979. Concurso Maria Canals, Barcelona.

112. "FONDATION MAEGHT" EXHIBITION. 1979. Fondation Maeght, Saint-Paul-de-Vence.

113. "HOMENATGE A GAUDÍ" EXHIBITION. 1979. Galeria Maeght, Barcelona.

114. "MIL LLIBRES EN CATALÀ". 1979. Edicions 62, Barcelona.

115. "ŒUVRES SUR PAPIER, PEINTURES, GRAPHIQUES" EXHIBITION. 1980. Isetan Museum, Tokyo.

116. "SERT-MIRÓ-FOIX-LLORENS ARTIGAS" EXHIBITION. 1980. Artema, Barcelona.

117. "MUSEO DE ARTE MODERNO DE MÉXICO" EXHIBITION. 1980. Museo de Arte Moderno, Mexico.

118. "HOMENATGE A J. TORRES CLAVE" EXHIBITION. 1980. Colegio de Arquitectos de Cataluña, Barcelona.

119. "60 VOLTA CICLISTA A CATALUNYA". 1980. Caixa de Pensions per a la Vellesa i d'Estalvis, Barcelona.

BIBLIOGRAPHY

BONNEFOY, Ives: *Miró*. Silvana Editoriale d'Arte, Milan, 1964.

CATALOGUE for the Exhibition "Joan Miró: Prints and Books", with texts by Evan H. Turner and Kneeland McNulty. Philadelphia Museum of Art. Philadelphia, 1966.

CATALOGUE for the Exhibition "Miró Barcelona 1968-1969", with texts by J. Ainaud de Lasarte and Francesc Vicens. Barcelona Town Council, Antiguo Hospital de la Santa Cruz. Ed. Polígrafa, S.A., Barcelona, 1968.

CATALOGUE for the Exhibition "Miró, l'oeuvre graphique", with texts by Jacques Lassaigne and Alexandre Cirici. Musée d'Art Moderne de la Ville de Paris, Paris, 1974.

CATALOGUE for the Exhibition "Joan Miró. Obra Gráfica", with text by Joan Teixidor. Ministry of Culture. Exhibition Halls of the Dirección General del Patrimonio Artístico, Archivos y Museos, Madrid, 1978.

CATALOGUE for the Exhibition "Joan Miró. Grafica", with texts by Aldo Cairola and Joan Teixidor. Palazzo Pubblico, Siena, May to September 1979.

CIRICI, Alexandre: *Miró llegit*. Edicions 62, Barcelona, 1971. Spanish version: *Miró en su obra*. Editorial Labor, Barcelona, 1970.
Miró Mirall. Ed. Polígrafa, S.A., Barcelona, 1977.

CHILO, Michel: *Miró, l'artiste et l'oeuvre*. Maeght éditeur, Paris, 1971.

DUPIN, Jacques: *Joan Miró: la vie et l'oeuvre*. Flammarion, Paris, 1961.

GIMFERRER, Pere: *Miró, colpir sense nafrar*. Ed. Polígrafa, S.A., Barcelona. Spanish version by the author, entitled: *Miró y su mundo*. Ed. Polígrafa, S.A., Barcelona, 1978.

HERRMANNS, Ralph: *Affischer av Miró*. A.H. Grafik, Stockholm, 1974.

HUNTER, Sam: *Joan Miró: das graphische Werk*. Hatje, Stuttgart, 1958. Spanish version: *Joan Miró. Su obra gráfica*. Ed. Gustavo Gili, S.A., Barcelona, 1959.

JOHANSSON, Kjell A.: *Miró en Escania*. "Dagens Nyheter", Stockholm, 30 June 1976.

LEIRIS, Michel and MOURLOT, Fernand: *Joan Miró lithographe I*. Maeght éditeur, Paris, 1972. Spanish version: *Joan Miró litógrafo I*. Ed. Polígrafa, S.A., Barcelona, 1972.

LOS PAPELES DE SON ARMADANS (monographic issue): *Joan Miró*. Madrid-Palma de Mallorca, Year II, Volume VII, No. XXI, 1957.

MOURLOT, Fernand: *Les affiches originales des maîtres de l'École de Paris: Braque, Chagall, Dufy, Léger, Matisse, Miró, Picasso*. André Sauret Éd., Montecarlo, 1959.

PENROSE, Roland: *Joan Miró*. The Arts Council of Great Britain, London, 1964.
Miró. Thames and Hudson, London, 1970. Spanish version: *Miró*. Daimon-Manuel Tamayo Editor, Barcelona, 1976.

QUENEAU, Raymond: *Joan Miró lithographe II*. Maeght éditeur, Paris, 1975. Spanish version: *Joan Miró litógrafo II*. Ed. Polígrafa, S.A., Barcelona, 1975.

RAILLARD, Georges: *Joan Miró. Ceci est la couleur de mes rêves*. Editions du Seuil, Paris. 1977. Spanish version: *Conversaciones con Joan Miró*. Granica Editor, Barcelona, 1978.

SOBY, James Thrall: *Joan Miró*. The Museum of Modern Art, New York, 1959. Spanish version: *Miró*. Universidad de Río Piedras, Puerto Rico.

TAILLANDIER, Yvon: *Miró à l'encre*. Spanish version: *Mirografías*. Ed. Gustavo Gili, S.A., Barcelona, 1972.

TEIXIDOR, Joan: *Joan Miró lithographe III*. Maeght éditeur, Paris, 1977. Spanish version: *Joan Miró litógrafo III*. Ed. Polígrafa, S.A., Barcelona, 1978.

WEMBER, Paul: *Miró das graphische Werk*. Kaiser Wilhelm Museum, Krefeld, 1957.

Printed in Spain by La Polígrafa, S. A. - Parets del Vallès (Barcelona) Spain - Dep. Legal: B. 25.429 - 1980